The Wings Of Freedom

In this age when the moral superiority of
a particular culture is determined on the basis
of its capacity to render nations powerful.

Laws, ethics, educations will remain
supreme to all beings.

Our world, should now become our push
towards social betterment.

This book is dedicated to my two Children
Teymor and Kar Shane Ilkin-Lee Hing

By Yildiz Ilkin

Author's Foreword

Canada is a great country, in historical timelines however it is still relatively new to the rest of the world. Today through the study of linguistic anthropology, social behavior's and our environment's role we are able to break perceptions and promote a different type of thinking. With our ultimate objective in pushing evolving to a completely different level. One with a global vision for advancing.

It starts with linguistic anthropology, a field of academia which is defined as the concept of analyzing languages first based on its chronology of order then extracting these words for anthropological use. This will aide us in collecting material first off by the use of descriptive narratives. How primitive man first saw the world or started primitively their developmental journey.

These narratives are critical in the study of early human social behaviors leading up to one person's vision of how we have not fully reached optimum levels of advancement. The attempt to understand radicalization of global languages, to that of what is human self-preservation behavioral dynamics. Merged with its basic functionality of economics and its vital role in pushing progress. The question is how do we attempt to create a state of equilibrium or what is healthy sustainability while comparing it to what went wrong historically?

Human advancement ultimately will be presented as the "finale series- called Let's Evolve" of a set of projected proposals of urban layout and pilot projects followed with ideas on progressive environmentalism at its ecosystem balance levels. What I call actually implementing our utopic world. continue

The capacity to blend existing with earth in a more maintainable way. Blue Mountain Mist starts the journey. It introduces many different areas of anthropological growth to deduce what went wrong historically, using my my multi-faceted background and years of hobby research of course!

Starting with shamanism as a connector point to all humans found globally and why humanity created such detrimental distinctions amongst themselves even amongst the human race. These poems link countries so that we can push progress. This stage is called the research or analysis slightly separated from the field of social studies called "social betterment".

What was a shaman, why was the culture of shaman hidden historically, the role of linguistics / religion and lastly breaking human identity perceptions in pushing the new dynamics of environmental thinking will now be our mandate? Taking advantage of our connections as humans in pushing green using my discovery of Kanata means Wings on July 1st, 2013.

These seven series presented below: are called *a different voice of reason or thinking*.

- ➢ *Blue Mountain Mist*

- ➢ *Animal To Hominid*

- ➢ *The Language Of Birds*

- ➢ *The Shamanic History Of Kanat*

- ➢ *The Venus Conversion*

- ➢ *Let's Evolve*

The practicality of a Yin female, and a planet in the healing."

Enjoy

Yildiz Ilkin

A Canadian Heritage Poem

Kana'da Tribe, Is This All Your Home?

We land on this land,

ice everywhere, its 1534.

Do you think they will like us?

Indian what is your name?

They don't answer, keep trying,

they don't answer,

I tell them mine.

Europe told us they are Kana people.

I think they are from Kana'da tribe.

Indian where is your home?

Pretend to do sleeping.

The land is cold,

our men are ghastly sick.

We need food,

danger lurks around us.

They point and say, "Kanat'a"

It looks like a small settlement.

We travel up north.

There are a hundred more,

Indian where are all of you from?

Their regions,

Hochelega, Iroquois, Oneida.

We must make way.

Europe is famish,

our people are hit with a plague,

we are so cold.

Our history says ugly,

we too have tribes and protect our own.

But tomorrow when we get stronger,

we will make way.

Yildiz Ilkin

I think of my ancestral departed,

the irony of a discovery that links

the meaning of the first of the family,

to the wings of past gone.

 Out of Africa came the shamanic word Kan,

The earliest meaning of the

blood of our ancestry.

Out of Anatolia and Early Asia

came Kan-at.

The wings that drew blood,

The evil Jin of our forefathers.

 Out of India came the Khans

An abbreviation of Khanat, as the

spirits in lead.

 Out of Israel, the wings throughout

the holy lands from before,

became their songs of Gush (kush).

Fifty thousands years ago

Canada also had Kanats,

but this time

a "protected" spiritual wing cover,

became a completely different

       change in cultural tune.

But it was out of Mongolia,

Genghis Khan who merged

his kingdom in four and

taught me history,

by far the most.

Call it the spirits of their past voice.

He said we rule as a mighty,

of all the territories we claim.

The Khans of East Asia,

merge them with the

Khanat's of Turkestan and that of

Khanat's of Persia,

lastly let the Khanat's of the

Golden Horde join in.

These are our wings of our

historical past.

But it was my grandpa who once said

 One hundred years ago, we picked Ilk-hans,
as the first of the family, these are the

clans of our own heritage to represent

an ancestral gift for generations of you.

                Yildiz Ilkin

Our Global Legacy, Shaman Was Thy Name!

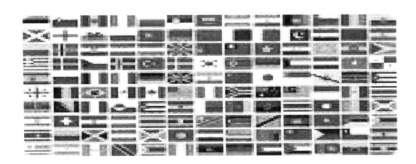

Private Note: *These poems were written while under house confinement for the last two years because of the request in releasing the content of the notes of my original work. famous became,* <u>*THE NOTES.*</u>

These poems were processed relatively quickly to introduce the project. Using accurate sources and very minimal fiction. Today I would now like to present to the world our ancestry. How it started, and that shamanism was once part of all our global name.

What is the critical importance of these poems? It illustrates our human connectivity in pushing progress, corporate ingenuity and green at its finest?

If there are any comments

Please can you email ilovelaw7@gmail.com

Notes for these poems can be found shortly on www.starilkin.com

Other Pages Of Interest www.vancats.com / http://oceanus12.wix.com/thefuture

Index

Argentina	The Argentina Republic	Our Elder Female	A16	43
Armenia	The Republic Of Armenia	Family We Became	A17	44
	Armenians Of Anatolia	The Ova Of Crosses	A18	45
	The Republic Of Armenia	See: By The Railway	C23	91
Aruba, Bonaire, Curacao	Kingdom Of Netherlands	Finding Heaven Underneath	A19	46
Australia	Commonwealth Of Australia	The Male Organ	A20	47
	Commonwealth Of Australia	Amata	A21	48
Austria	Republic Of Austria	Earth's Keeper I am	A22	48
Azerbaijan	The Republic Of Azerbaijan	The Elements of Fire	A23	49

Section B

Name Of Country	Official Regional Title	Poem Title	Code ID	Page
Bahamas	The Commonwealth Of The Bahamas	Baby Blue Crystal Glass	B1	51
Bahrain	The Kingdom Of Bahrain	Meaningful Female	B2	52
Bangladesh	People's Republic Of Bangladesh	Bengal Tiger	B3	53
Barbados	Barbados	The Little Boy And His Bridge	B4	54
Belarus	Republic Of Belarus	The Beloved Aya	B5	55
Belgium	Kingdom Of Belgium	How God's Tears Made The Rivers	B6	56
Belize	Belize	Dear Spirits	B7	57
Benin	The Republic Of Benin	Spirits Of Africa	B8	58

Bhutan	The Kingdom Of Bhutan	Clean Spirited Soul	B9	59
Bolivia	Republic Of Bolivia	The Landing Point Tiwanaku	B10	60
Bonaire	Kingdom's Island Of Bonaire	See Finding Heaven Underneath	A19	46
Bosnia And Herzegovina	Republic Of Bosnia And Herzegovina	Mehmet Pasha	B11	61
Botswana	The Republic Of Botswana	Running Free With The Herd	B12	62
Brazil	Brazil	Pink River Dolphin	B13	63
Brunei	Brunei Darussalam	Sultanate	B14	64
Bulgaria	Republic Of Bulgaria	God's Gift	B15	65
	Republic Of Bulgaria	Proverb	B16	66
	Republic Of Bulgaria	See: Beyond The River Hebrus	H4	153
Burkina Faso	Burkina Faso	A World Once Before	B17	67
Burundi	The Republic Of Burundi	The Mountains	B18	68

Section C

Name Of Country	Official Regional Title	Poem Title	Code ID	Page
Cambodia	The Kingdom Of Cambodia	Angkor	C1	70
Cameroon	The Republic Of Cameroon	Wah-za National Park	C2	71
Canada	Canada	Patriotic Heart	C3	72
	Canada	Canada's New Skyline	C4	73
	Canada	I Stole The Apple From The Bee	C5	74
	Canada	Shaman Was My Name	C6	75

	Canada	The Bering Confusion	C7	76
	Canada	Turkish Girl	C8	77
	Canada	White Negro Child	C9	78
	Canada	C'est La Vie	C10	79
	Canada	What Has The Blues Given	C11	80
Cape Verde	The Republic Of Cape Verde	The Isles Off Africa	C12	81
Central African Republic	The Central African Republic	Chari River	C13	82
Central Asia	Central Asia	The Shamanic Prayer	C14	83
	Central Asia	The Stans Of Central Asia	C15	84
	Central Asia	See Battle After Battle, They Became	A6	33
Chad	The Republic Of Chad	Quilted Tapestry	C16	85
Chile	Republic Of Chile	The Black Mummy	C17	86
China	The People's Republic Of China	Cave Person	C18	87
	The People's Republic Of China	Dark Fairy Mountains	C19	88
	The People's Republic Of China	Proverb	C20	88
	The People's Republic Of China	Your Majesty	C21	89
Clans of Southern Turkey	Region Clans OF Southern Turkey	Blue Eyes	C22	90
Colombia	The Republic Of Colombia	By The Railway	C23	91
Comoros	The Union Of The Comoros	The Essence Of Vanilla	C24	92

Congo, Democratic Republic	The Democratic Republic Of The Congo	Congo's Genocide	C25	93
Congo, Republic The	People's Republic Of Congo	Teke, The Minority Is This Tribe	C26	94
Costa Rica	The Republic Of Costa Rica	Tropical Nights	C27	95
Cote D'Ivoire	The Republic Of Cote D'Ivoire	Pygmy Hippopotamus	C28	96
Croatia	Republic Of Croatia	Wild Horse	C29	97
Cuba	The Republic Of Cuba	Oh How I Love The Cuban People	C30	98
Curacao	Curacao (2005)	See Finding Heaven Underneath	A19	46
Cyprus	The Republic Of Cyprus	Run My Loved Ones	C31	99
Czech Republic	Czech Republic	Christ's Halo	C32	100

Section D

Name Of Country	Official Regional Title	Poem Title	Code ID	Page
Denmark	Kingdom Of Denmark	The Cultural Touch	D1	102
	Kingdom Of Denmark	The Nissum Fjord	D2	103
Djibouti	The Republic Of Djibouti	The Market In Djibouti	D3	104
Dominica	Commonwealth Of Dominica	Boiling Lake	D4	105
Dominican Republic	The Dominican Republic	War Of Independence	D5	106

Section E

Name Of Country	Official Regional Title	Poem Title	Code ID	Page
Ecuador	Republic Of Ecuador	Almost Human	E1	108
Egypt	Arab Republic Of Egypt	The Spirit Of Tutankhamen	E2	109
	Arab Republic Of Egypt	The Warrior Known As Musa	E3	110
El Salvador	The Republic Of El Salvador	Spectrum Of Light	E4	111
Equatorial Guinea	The Republic Of Equatorial Guinea	The Fang Chief Said	E5	112
Eritrea	Eritrea	The Admiration Of Aksumite Empire	E6	113
Estonia	Republic Of Estonia	The Transformation of Tallinn	E7	114
Ethiopia	Federal Democratic Republic Of Ethiopia	Kingdom Of Kush	E8	115
Etruscan Territories	Etruscan Territories	Moon Dance	E9	116
Eurasia	Eurasia, Territory	Two Wild Horses	E10	117
Europe	Europe	The Birth Of Satan	E11	118
	Europe	The Group OF White Knights	E12	119
	Europe	The Private Race Of Man	E13	120

Section F

Name Of Country	Official Regional Title	Poem Title	Code ID	Page
Fiji	Sovereign Democratic Republic Of The Fiji Islands	Paradise Cove	F1	122

	Sovereign Democratic Republic Of The Fiji Islands	Kula Eco- Park	F2	122
Finland	Republic Of Finland	The Boy And His Lantern	F3	123
France	French Republic	Fontainebleau	F4	124
	French Republic	The Breaking Of Human Distinction	F5	125
	French Republic	Nuit Noir	F6	126
France, Normandy	French Republic	The Battle Beyond D-DAY	F7	127
French Guiana	The Department OF Guyane	Historical	F8	128

Section G

Name Of Country	Official Regional Title	Poem Title	Code ID	Page
Gabon	The Republic Of Gabon	A spoon Made From Food	G1	130
Gambia	The Republic Of The Gambia	By Gambia's River	G2	131
Georgia	Republic Of Georgia	Why Are The God's Crying	G3	132
Germany	The Federal Republic Of Germany	Bird In The Wind	G4	133
	The Federal Republic Of Germany	Aachen Catheral	G5	134
	Historical	Saint Ursula	G5	134
Ghana	The Republic Of Ghana	The Struggle Of Women	G6	135
	The Republic Of Ghana	See Slave Route	A13	40
Global	Global	Earth Became My Zoo	G7	136

	Global	A Secret	G8	137
	Global	I Grip Your Head Tight	G9	138
	Global	Whose Monkey Is The Better Monkey?	G10	139
Greece	The Hellenic Republic	The Greek Goddess	G11	140
	The Hellenic Republic	Konyaliyim	G12	141
	The Hellenic Republic	The Skatan	G13	142
	The Hellenic Republic	A Mix of Three, We Became Thee	G14	143
Greenland	Greenland	The Fight For Artic	G15	144
Grenada	Grenada	New Grenada	G16	145
Guam	Guam	Chukchi Nomads Of Guam	G17	146
Guatemala	The Republic Of Guatemala	I Love God	G18	146
Guinea	The Republic Of Guinea	Guinea Fowl	G19	147
Guinea- Bissau	The Republic Of Guinea-Bissau	Traditional African Religion	G20	148
Guyana	Co-operative Republic Of Guyana	Sleep Peacefully Mama	G21	149

Section H

Name Of Country	Official Regional Title	Poem Title	Code ID	Page
Haiti	The Republic Of Haiti	The Red Voodoo	H1	151
	The Republic Of Haiti	Proverb	H2	151
Hattusa, Hittite	Territory	The Secret	H3	152

Empire		Lines		
Hebrus River, Surroundings	Territory	Beyond The River Hebrus	H4	153
Honduras, Barbados, Panama	The Republic Of Honduras	Captain Sir Henry Morgan	H5	154
Hungary	Republic Of Hungary	Counting Sheep	H6	155

Section I

Name Of Country	Official Regional Title	Poem Title	Code ID	Page
Iceland	The Republic Of Iceland	The Dolls Of Iceland	I1	157
India	Republic Of India	Ram Is My Kar	I2	158
	Republic Of India	The Revolution	I3	159
	Republic Of India	Sanskrit	I4	159
	Republic Of India	Ignore Monogamy	I5	160
	Republic Of India	Sun Temple Konarak	I6	161
	Republic Of India	See: Hindu Kush	P1	241
Indonesia	Republic Of Indonesia	The Living	I7	162
Iran	The Islamic Republic Of Iran	Assassin	I8	163
	The Islamic Republic Of Iran	The Three Prayers And One Sacrifice of Elam	I9	164
Iraq	Republic Of Iraq	Feeding The Sun God	I10	165
	Republic Of Iraq	Ottoman Head Quarters	I11	166
	Republic Of Iraq	Tribal We Are	I12	167
	Republic Of Iraq	Uri	I13	168
Ireland	Eire (Republic	Castle On	I14	169

		Of Ireland)	Inishmore		
Israel	The State Of Israel	Adam or …..	I15	170
	The State Of Israel	Ahu'di	I16	171
	The State Of Israel	The Elder of Safad	I17	172
	The State Of Israel	The White Lion Of Golan Heights	I18	173
	The State Of Israel	Yehudi	I19	174
	The State Of Israel	The Seven Day War	I20	175
	The State Of Israel	The Warrior Known As Musa	E3	110
	The State Of Israel	See: Homage to Yacoub Aga	L7	195
Italy	The Republic Of Italy	Marco Polo	I21	176
	The Republic Of Italy	Roma's Mark	I22	177
	The Republic Of Italy	See: Columbus Said	S26	283

Section J

Name Of Country	Official Regional Title	Poem Title	Code ID	Page
Jamaica	Jamaica	Proverb	J1	179
	Jamaica	Bob Marley	J2	179
Japan	Japan	Osaka	J3	180
	Japan	Shintoism	J4	180
Jordan	The Hashemite Kingdom Of Jordan	Dry River Valley	J5	181

Section K

Name Of Country	Official Regional Title	Poem Title	Code ID	Page
Kazakhstan	Republic Of Kazakhstan	Dark Wings, Black Nights	K1	183

Kenya	The Republic Of Kenya	Hours Spent Studying Fingers And Skies	K2	184
Kiribati	Republic Of Kirbati	Magical Phoenix	K3	185
Kosovo	Kosovo	The Ova Of Birds	K4	185
Kuwait	State Of Kuwait	Tragedy Of Life	K5	186
Kyrgyzstan	Republic Of Kyrgyzstan	The Poet	K6	187

Section L

Name Of Country	Official Regional Title	Poem Title	Code ID	Page
Laos	Lao People's Democratic Republic	The One Million Elephants	L1	189
Latvia	Republic Of Latvia	Walk Along With Me	L2	190
Lebanon	The Republic Of Lebanon	Roman Style	L3	191
Lesotho		What Is Death	L4	192
Liberia	The Republic Of Liberia	Graveyard	L5	193
Libya	The Socialist People's Libyan Arab Jumhuriya	Tour Guide To Tourist	L6	194
Libya to Ukraine	The Historical Coastal Line Walkway	Homage to Yacoub Aġa	L7	195
Liechtenstein	Principality Of Liechtenstein	Liechtenstein	L8	196
Lithuania	Republic Of Lithuania	Follow The Path Of Light	L9	197
Luxembourg	Grand Duchy Of Luxembourg	House Of Burgundy	L10	198

Section M

Name Of Country	Official Regional Title	Poem Title	Code ID	Page
Macedonia	The Former Yugoslav	In Search Of Sanctuary	M1	200

	Republic Of Macedonia			
Madagascar	The Republic Of Madagascar	Movement Of First Words	M2	201
Malawi	The Republic Of Malawi	Bettering Thy Self	M3	202
Malaysia	Malaysia	The Language Of Birds	M4	203
Maldives	The Republic Of Maldives	Stars Of The Indian Ocean	M5	203
Mali	The Republic Of Mali	Emperor of Songhai	M6	204
Malta	Republic Of Malta	The Purpose Of All The Prophets	M7	205
Marshall Islands	The Republic Of Marshall Islands	White Star	M8	206
Mauritania	The Republic Of Mauritania	Cross The Gibraltar	M9	207
Mauritius	Republic Of Mauritius	The Extinct Dodo Bird	M10	208
	Republic Of Mauritius	Historical	M11	208
Mesopotamia & North Africa	Territory	Babi-illim Our Watchtower (Babylon)	M12	209
Mesopotamian Region	Region	Transformed Fig Leaf	M13	210
Mexico	United States Of Mexico	The Collapse Of Mayan	M14	211
	United States Of Mexico	Proverb	M15	212
Micronesia	Federated States Of Micronesia	Agana	M16	212
Moldova	Republic Of Moldova	The Meat Of A Walnut	M17	213
Monaco	Principality Of Monaco	Honour Thyself	M18	214
Mongolia	Mongolia	Centre Of The Hunic Empire	M19	215
Montenegro	Montenegro	Black Mountains	M20	216

Morocco	The Kingdom Of Morocco	Gua, Hua, Dua	M21	217
Mozambique	Republic Of Mozambique	Portuguese Maritime Routes	M22	218
Myanmar (Burma)	Union Of Myanmar	Unpolluted In Our Spiritual Ways	M23	219

Section N

Name Of Country	Official Regional Title	Poem Title	Code ID	Page
Namibia, South Africa	The Republic Of Namibia	The Beauty Of Raw	N1	221
Nauru	The Republic Of Nauru	Don't You Ever Lose The Fight	N2	222
Nepal	Nepal	Mountains Of Pain	N3	223
Netherlands, The	Kingdom Of The Netherlands	Masters Of The Virgo	N4	224
New Zealand	New Zealand	The Flightless Bird	N5	225
	New Zealand	Historical	N6	225
	New Zealand	The Mythical Land Whanganata	N7	226
Nicaragua	The Republic Of Nicaragua	Niii They Screeched	N8	227
Niger	The Republic Of Niger	The Aga Of The Region	N9	227
Nigeria	The Federal Republic Of Nigeria	White-Face Painted, African Tribe	N10	228
North Africa	North Africa Territory	Negroid	N11	229
	North Africa Territory	See Battle After Battle, They Became	A6	33

	North Africa Territory	See: Babi-illim Our Watchtower (Babylon)	M12	209
North Africa, The Arabian Peninsula, Israel	North Africa, The Arabian Peninsula, Israel	Bedouin Indigenous Female	N10	230
North America's Native	North American Continent	Forested Shaman	N11	231
	North American Continent	Great Spirit In The Sky	N12	232
	North American Continent	Proverb	N13	233
	North American Continent	Man, Women And Child	N14	234
North Korea	Democratic People's Republic Of Korea	Blessings & Misfortunes	N15	235
	Democratic People's Republic Of Korea	Historical	N16	235
Norway	Kingdom Of Norway	Darkness And Ice	N17	236
	Kingdom Of Norway	The Nor-Way Is The Path	N18	237

Section O

Name Of Country	Official Regional Title	Poem Title	Code ID	Page
Oman	Sultanate Of Oman	The 21 Tombs	O1	239

Section P

Name Of Country	Official Regional Title	Poem Title	Code ID	Page
Pakistan, Northern to India	The Islamic Republic Of Pakistan	The Kafirs of Hindu Kush	P1	241
	The Islamic Republic Of Pakistan	The Region Of Kashmir	P2	241
Palau	The Republic Of Palau	Proverb	P3	242
Palestine	The Palestinian Territories	We Are First Clan	P4	243
Panama	Republic Of Panama	Green Canopy	P5	244
	Republic Of Panama	Captain Sir Henry Morgan	H5	154
Papua New Guinea	The Independent State Of Papua New Guinea	The Lord Of The Flies	P6	245
Paraguay	The Republic Of Paraguay	Indigenous We Are	P7	246
Peru	Republic Of Peru	Peruvian	P8	247
Philippines	Republic Of The Philippines	Non-Believer	P9	248
Poland	The Republic Of Poland	The Churches Of Peace	P10	249
	The Republic Of Poland	See: The Beloved Aya	B5	55
Portugal	Portuguese Republic	Faith	P11	250

Section Q

Name Of Country	Official Regional Title	Poem Title	Code ID	Page
Qatar	State Of Qatar	The Royal Tribe, Bani Tamim	Q1	252

Section R

Name Of Country	Official Regional Title	Poem Title	Code ID	Page

Romania	Republic Of Romania	Drakula	R1	254
	Republic Of Romania	Proverb	R2	254
Russia	Russian Federation	Catherine The Great	R3	255
	Russian Federation	Historical	R4	226
	Russian Federation	The Passageway Of Energy	R5	226
Russia, Yakut	Russian Federation	The Circle Of Life	R6	257
Rwanda	The Republic Of Rwanda	Fierce Child	R7	258

Section S

Name Of Country	Official Regional Title	Poem Title	Code ID	Page
Sahara Region	Sahara Region	The Drastic Mistake Of Early Man	S1	260
Saint Kitts And Nevis	The Federation Of Saint Kitts And Nevis	Caribs	S2	261
Saint Lucia	Saint Lucia	The Volcanoes That Spoke	S3	262
Saint Vincent And The Grenadines	Saint Vincent And The Grenadines	Amerindian Worship	S4	263
Samoa	The Independent State Of Samoa	Tutuila	S5	264
San Marino	The Most Serene Republic Of San Marino	Ave Maria	S6	265
Sao Tome And Principe	The Democratic Republic Of Sao Tome And Principe	The Land Made Me	S7	266

Saudi Arabia	Kingdom Of Saudi Arabia	We Apologize	S8	267
Scandinavian Countries - South Africa to The Sahara Belt	Territories	In The Battle Of Life	S9	268
	Territories	In The Battle Of Life	S10	268
Senegal	The Republic Of Senegal	Dances of Life	S11	269
Serbia	Republic Of Serbia	Stari Ras	S12	270
Seychelles	Republic Of Sychelles	Historical	S13	271
Sierra Leone	The Republic Of Sierra Leone	Raven's In The Sky	S14	272
Singapore	Republic Of Singapore	My Motto Is Balance	S15	273
	Republic Of Singapore	Our Indian Prince	S16	274
Slovakia	Slovak Republic	Is There A God?	S17	275
Slovenia	Republic Of Slovenia	The Stilt Houses Of Slovenia	S18	276
Solomon Islands	Soloman Islands	Darkness	S19	277
Somalia	Somalia	Shaman You Are, Shaman I am	S20	278
South Africa	Republic Of South Africa	In the Light Of The Sun	S21	279
	Republic Of South Africa	See: The Beauty Of Raw	N1	221
	Republic Of South Africa	See: In the Battle Of Life	S3	262
	Republic Of South Africa	See: In The Battle Of Life	S9	263

South Korea	The Republic Of Korea	Many Moons Ago	S22	280
South Sudan	South Sudan	Historical	S23	281
Spain	The Kingdom Of Spain	The Sons Of Darkness	S24	281
	The Kingdom Of Spain	Ci or Si or Sea?	S25	282
	The Kingdom Of Spain	Columbus Said	S26	283
Sri Lanka	The Democratic Socialist Republic Of Sri Lanka	The Flying Goddess	S27	284
Sudan	Republic Of Sudan	They Asked Nubia	S28	285
Suriname	The Republic Of Suriname	Historical	S29	286
Swaziland	The Kingdom Of Swaziland	The Great River Of Usutu	S30	286
Sweden	Kingdom Of Sweden	Make you Laugh Some More	S31	287
	Kingdom Of Sweden	Sweden's Christmases	S32	288
Switzerland	Swiss Confederation	Dedicated To Human	S33	289
	Swiss Confederation	Alp Is Still Thy Name	S34	290
Syria	The Arab Republic Of Syria	Proverb	S35	291
	The Arab Republic Of Syria	The Shamans of Su'Riya	S36	291

Section T

Name Of Country	Official Regional Title	Poem Title	Code ID	Page
Taiwan	Republic Of China	Ilha Formosa	T1	293
Tajikistan	Republic Of Tajikistan	Tadzik	T2	293

Tanzania	The United Republic Of Tanzania	Tan Tan Goes The Gods	T3	294
	The United Republic Of Tanzania	Spirits Of Past Life	T4	295
Thailand	Kingdom Of Thailand	Buddhism	T5	296
Timor- Leste	Democratic Republic Of Timor- Leste	The Black Triangle	T6	297
Togo	The Republic Of Togo	The Constant Of Vocal	T7	297
Tonga	Kingdom Of Tonga	The Summit Of Volcano	T8	298
Trinidad And Tobago	Republic Of Trinidad And Tobago	Young Coconut Jelly	T9	299
Tunisia	The Republic Of Tunisia	The Amphitheatre	T10	300
Turkey	The Republic Of Turkey	Hagia Sophia	T11	301
	Turkey	The Hidden Underground	T12	302
	Turkey	Isyanbul- Istanbul	T13	303
	Turkey	The Victims, Of The End Of War	T14	304
	Turkey	See Konyaliyim	G12	141
Turkic Countries	Turkic Countries	Educate, Some More?	T15	305
Turkmenistan	The Republic Of Turkmenistan	Earthquake	T16	306
Tuvalu	The Constitutional Moarchy Of Tuvalu	The Spanish Explorer	T17	307

Section U

Name Of Country	Official Regional Title	Poem Title	Code ID	Page
Uganda	The Republic Of Uganda	The Gods	U1	309
Ukraine	Ukraine	Titanium	U2	310
	Ukraine	See: Homage to Yacoub Aga	L7	195
United Arab Emirates	United Arab Emirates	Evil Spirits	U3	311
United Kingdom	United Kingdom Of Great Britain And Northern Ireland	Evolutionary Difficulties	U4	312
	United Kingdom Of Great Britain And Northern Ireland	The Lady With The Lamp	U5	313
	United Kingdom Of Great Britain And Northern Ireland	The Light Of Europe	U6	314
	United Kingdom Of Great Britain And Northern Ireland	Historical	U7	315
United States	United States Of America	Alpha Quadrant	U8	316
	United States Of America	Kokopelli Tribe	U9	317
	United States Of America	The Other Side Of War	U10	318
	United States Of America	Stuck At The Border	U11	319
	United States Of America	Apache	U12	320
United States, New York	United States Of America	Manhattan	U13	321
United States,	United States	I Am The	U14	322

Los Angeles	Of America	Fallen Angel Lucifer		
Uruguay	The Oriental Republic Of Uruguay	The Poisonous Shells	U15	323
Uzbekistan	The Republic Of Uzbekistan	The Moon In The Day	U16	324

Section V

Name Of Country	Official Regional Title	Poem Title	Code ID	Page
Vanuatu	The Republic Of Vanuatu	Roi Mata	V1	326
Vatican City	The State OF The Vatican City aka The Holy See	Homage To The Sky	V2	326
Venezuela	The Bolivarian Republic Of Venezuela	Caracas	V3	327
Vietnam	The Socialist Republic Of Vietnam	Listen Only To Your Inner Soul	V4	328

Section Y

Name Of Country	Official Regional Title	Poem Title	Code ID	Page
Yemen	Republic Of Yemen	Al- Yaman	Y1	330

Section Z

Name Of Country	Official Regional Title	Poem Title	Code ID	Page
Zambia	The Republic Of Zambia	The Highest	Z1	332
Zimbabwe	The Republic Of Zimbabwe	Kariba	Z2	333

A1- Afghanistan

Bãmiãn Valley We lost another artefact, tears we cry today. A Buddhist monastic symbol. Heritage early man so easily for took. Not understanding the prayers it laid. And how lively and commerce filled the region was when Western Turks and Genghis Khan once ruled. Part of our shamanic Gandhara art. Gone are the hands that took hours to make. Massive mountains carved one millimetre at a time. The century of chisel by primitively sharpened tools. When earth becomes fully human, we will build it again one day.	 Gone Today

A2- Afghanistan

We are managed by the Persian Achaemenian empire and have just met the wrath of Alexander III the Great.	

29

We Say Ruh!

We bang hard on his chest
Ruh
He is not coming back
Ruh
We mourn around him
Ruh
We shake our heads
Ruh
Hear our animal sounds
Ruh
We now understand
he is with the ones flying.

The land, the spirits, the masks, and
straw dresses. Where proto-Turkic
Afrikaans our first migratory out, known
as our global shamanic history out of
Africa was born.

Ruh

Hand of Animal

Balkan Traveler

Balkan regional friend.
You come tired to this
town called Berat.

Part of your Ottoman heritage too.
It speaks to us about
the many things we
may have missed of our past.

Vacant it sits alone,
on this very mountain top.
How our early humans
prayed.

The 13th century citadel.
That stands tall and protected today,
was designs so typically the same
to that of its era.

First floors are for the freezing
cold months they huddled.
The second floor for the breezy
love making of
summers that once had slipped by.

Balkan traveler stand very still
and quiet, in this old kule.
And listen carefully to those like you
who once had passed by.

Berat and Gjirokastra Centre

Kasbah of Algeria

The many worlds of Africa,
exotic and ancient.

Centuries of ancestors ago.
Bâh, our shamans would first
attempt to make vocal for cover.

Our earliest designated feeding points.
The fierce power and muscle.
They called the region, that their
many Gods who stole lives.

Phoenician trading posts,
their temporary resting place.
Evolved it to become
the center points of
protected town living.

Ottoman style palaces
became transformed again.
A deep rooted community,
of honour and Islamic teachings.

Kasbah your winding streets
and ancient alleys.

Made north Africa our first
real civilizations of life.

The Waterfalls Of Life

Battle After Battle, They Became

The Byzantium Splendour

Christian, Muslim, Jew we house all,
to Persia we reach.
Except our lead and save life.
Gold, you must pay.
We will not pull a strife.

The Mongolian Empire Monarch

Earthly shamanic we are;
to Ankara we reach.
Except our empire and save life.
Feed us, you must pay.
Understand our severe ways.

The Ottoman Grandeur

Christian, Muslim, Jew and more,
we all are.
Twenty-four countries we reach.
Except us and save life.
Honour us, or death will be your fate.

This is a must for each one of us,
understand we stand tall.

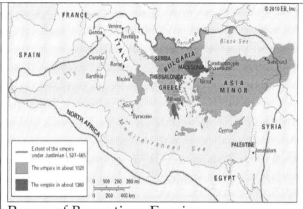

Range of Byzantium Empire

The Rabbi & His Goose

The Rabbi with his rosy red cheeks,
on the way to the open market
near Balat, found an injured
baby goose.

Come home with me.
Let me feed you something to eat,
and help you fix your injury.

But first let's take five minutes
to sit in this dreadful heat.
The flowing water by the stream
will cool both of us down.
While I check everything.

You can roam in our small garden,
and I do love animals do not fear.
Just provide some eggs
and we will make sure other
animals stay clear.

The white goose that day onward
followed the Rabbi everywhere
he went.

The Rabbi & His Goose

Spain's Persecution

Hear ye, hear ye
oh great Sultan,
they desperately need your
help.

The year is 1453,
Spain is after us.
Torn are our shoes,
barefoot we wail.

Send the ships
Immediately.
Hardship looms over
the many, their message
echoes through.

The harbour boats,
they wait.
One at a time they arrive,
thousands of nautical miles
from home.

"You stay with us", the Ottoman's say,
Born were you from our regions,
you belong to us Yerusha people.

Filled with honour like us.
Let those find God,
who harm you.

*"You will find peace in our
regions".*

The Ottomans, once had said.

*Ottoman ships picking up Jews in Spain in
1453, also known as the expulsion of Jews
called
by anti-Semitic Pedro Sarmiento Converso.*

Two Goats On A Bridge

Elders would tell many
stories to teach the young.
Here is another that was,
happily, sung.

Two goats attempted to
cross the narrow bridge.
Both said move,
so I can have first dibs.

As they fought and
headed each other,
both fell off and died
in a fretted mutter.

The moral of the story
is simple you see.
While we bicker about
our shamanic history
and the dialogues of
our first.

Earth is missing a lot,
especially in quenching
thirst.
> Being the wisest of the wise.
> We can use Native ideology and
> the discovery of wings to push
> progress and be green.
> The lessons of these goats
> should now be remembered
> by us historically.

Politics is politics but
academia always comes first.
Unlike the other two goats
in the fable, pretty equal in size.

If you don't see the rays of academia
our prism of sky blue light as way bigger.
Even with political disguise,
We may all fall off and die.
Surrender please and move aside.

Historic Fables Of The Region

The Princess Who Marked Her Name

Our forefathers once lived,
in early darkness,
in animal hide tents.

At the base of the mountains
they would lean up against
the large boulders to naturally
protect against those that caused
cold.

They would ask the highest,
Anie peak.
Give us another story.
The feminine spirits would gently
respond back.

Of how Pyrene the mighty,
gave birth to a serpent.
And she would then run away into the
woods.
Afraid that her father, the earthly giant
would be angry.

Alone, she would pour out her heart
felt story to the trees and their
surroundings.
But this time attracting the attention
of wild beasts who tore her to pieces.

Are you afraid our forefathers would
ask?
Only to find the children had
quickly fallen asleep.

Snuggled five in a row, under heavy
pounds
of leathery-fur pull.
The only item to protect against dreadful
colds.
The covers neatly scraped
and washed with palm comfortable
rocks.

The passing of time our early humans
first attempted to do.
In the months of months of subzero cold
and the human resilient will
to get through.

The Princess Pyrene

The Lion And The Bird

Landscape saturation over time
means a relationship.
Our ecosystems even developed
species variant animal friendships.

The little bird one day pecked
at the lion's rear in his territory
at the base of the river basin
Okavango.

The lion look ferociously,
this bird must be insane
and giggled what the hell
is this near?

Something went funny
he got a peck more.
But enjoyed the kiss of the
unwanted host that rode.

Like the hippo and the crocodile,
they too became inseparable mates.

This is a story of politics we know
is a hidden secret using the case
of the lion and his little mate.

The Lion And His Mate

Irishmen We Are

Ulster was our region,
back home.

The wild wolf and the stars
symbolizes where we came from.

In 1688 we came to
Anguilla and just took.

An empty acre of flat land,
where our shamrocks can be found.

The sound of ocean tide every time
the wind blew, made it an awesome
living ground!

Irish we are, Anguilla became our
second land.

Irish We Are!

Slave Route

Africa has no history, no memory
no castles or forts.
As far as we are concern they
don't even have humans.
The captain spoke.

The death ships arrived one by one.
Their past history, became what is
known as the emergence of fire.
The earliest chronical of Antiguan
abhorrence to the injustices of faith.
The slashing of raw flesh on barb wire.

The Amerindians first hesitantly came to
shore, they presented a circle in a flat
chiseled marked stone.
Life, silence, sharing, respect it showed.
Our tribes give it to those we encounter
first. Their attempt to be pleasantly bold.

Flipped off their hands the foreigners
did. Our historical past tells us of the
injured spirits, that once were the same
scenes overseas.

But some islands became uniquely hated,
by the masters themselves.
This history dictates to us so very well.
Antigua is one, with a majestic sounding
of conch horn, to alarm all the bells.

They were the blood of Ghana warriors
(part of several groups of Kana tribes),
these slaves rebelled continuously,
The island that now became known as the
beautiful 14-mile zone from hell.

At first conquest something interesting
 history hides from others, this must be
told. Slaves and island inhabitant through
base understanding became the wild
barbarians, that first became unified
against all their foes.

Drastically sick became the locals and the
first to go. Their spirits back those at war.

But it was the negro who endured the
longest torment and torture. The bone
grinder it was known did not persuade
differently any of their anguish and
despair.

We will turn this entire island into a
fortress the nightly private talks were
held. We will exterminate all white
populations.
We are not like the others; their grunting
can still be heard echoing through the
tides swell.

"Ghana chiefs"
They pounded heavily on their chest!
Ocean salt, mixed blood with sweat.
That heavily came down.

Proud is the blood of our
ancestry we carry.
"Death till we are free"
We will never have any boundaries.

They circled barefoot with sticks, the
island sandy floor. Holding it against the
inevitable counterattack, island visits
started to slow.

Antigua to be remembered by its proud
slave rebellion name. The earliest visuals
of labelling what was a foreign window
frame of misery.

Human Locks

How Spoiled We Are

Many things in this world
we take for granted!
Voltage power,
running tap water
and our high towers.

For many centuries,
a toilet was
the left side of the creek.
What we called a tributary
water outlet.

The settling of early humans
in-between a vee, where one
side became to eat and the other
side became the raw hand of wipe,
and to leak.

No heat.
The grounds were dug
four feet deep.
And animals were put
in circular position where they
could all sleep.

When the mountains whistled
and temperatures fell at -50 below.
The story changed to struggle
and the unbearableness of the
extremity of no heat.
Something fascinating happened,
part of our animal kingdom narration of
environmental scuffle.

Early humans to prevent
freezing slept in the middle.
Called the survival huddled.
The animal breath and the smell of feces
really did not matter.
The life of human became what is creative
endurance. The story of, are we going to
exist one more day, the surroundings our
dreadful rival.

Integrated we are with the living.
Little do we know how hard it
was for early human survival.

Picture is an old depiction of the city of Kars.
An old Armenian village creatively designed
and placed westerly-wind protected on a
mountain side, was part of an independent
kingdom known as Vannad.

She Was Made In Ararat

Made were you in bliss but
the souls of her past was
imprinted onto her
mother's womb.

The conception that became a
life lasting of sensory of pain.

Even before you were born
your purpose came to light.
The transfer of the forgotten,
called the spirit of past ghosts.

The mountains of centuries,
were always known by our
forefathers as lethal in disguise.

For every tear, that existed on its slopes
suffering transformed you.
A wretched mark on your soul.

The hiding point known as the
mountains of aches.

 The once lethal peaks
nowadays lights up at its base
with a glimmer of life.

Our ancestry, is the highlight.
Many changes have been made.
But the mountains of pain,
are still its famous name.

Ararat Mountains

Our Elder Female

Your beautiful skin
untold by the marks
of life.

Even when you scratch
your face,
to show others
the immense pain
of an incident unfolded.

A womb ripped with
shreds of sweat.
You are proud of your age
showing all your beautiful
grey tussles.

Refusing even root dye or
henna.
The realism of a genuine women,
indigenous and proud yet
never forgotten.

As an elder female,
you have given your life
for those up to seven generations
after you.

Elder Female

Family We Became

Almond shape are our eyes,
A beautiful light bronze was
our skin.
They once quietly said,
You are brothers of our men
You are brothers of our men

Alphabet is closest to that
of the cradle, Ethiopia.
You are brothers of our men
You are brothers of our men

We permanently mark our women,
for decor.
You are brothers of our men
You are brothers of our men
We too are shamanic, by surprise.
You are brothers of our men
You are brothers of our men

Forefathers of Byzantium, Hurrian,
Ottoman and the many before us
were the tribes, that made the fabric
of us.

Men, who became our ancestral
pride. Culture is our heritage,
life that became ingrained in us.

We now happily sing.
Mother first, you made all of us.
We now understand our tribes, one
of our oldest recorded by
Damascus first.
We are really only brothers
of your men.
Brothers of your men.

Armaeans Indigenous Women

The Ova Of Crosses

Southern Turkey, contains
a dark secret.
The bodies of thousands.

Quietly buried but not
forgotten.
Call it our gruesome past.

Some say Ottoman infractions,
the other half,
yells "blatant murder and a
systematically ghastliest task".

The harshest decisions
parents had to make.
"*Give us some of your ancestry
or all of you die at the stake*".

To appease the local women
who wailed,
leave the innocence please.
Many children, each family took.
Young girls were married off quick.

One by one, the Ova of crosses
represented
the life given back to earth.
Of the regions they called heritage.
A genocide of war, and a no mercy
on the human core.

A shatter of a heart shaped glass.
The study of many atrocities
should make humanity think
about our past.

Does it really matter,
the change we can't revive?
What went wrong and the reincarnation
of life that disappeared?

We should all say, *"study these early human
atrocities and push human consciousness to
the level of extreme"*.

This is humanities new social ethics and
the
remembrance of the spirits that were
once seen.

Ova Of Crosses

Finding Heaven Underneath

A small crack of sunlight
in the sky.
On the boat I stand,
the salt water touches
my lips.

Captain which point will
you stop?
A few nautical miles south,
Bellafonte's Isle.

At first doesn't seem like
much.
But mermaid I be.
Jump nude in the water
what a sight, I now see?

Blue parrot fishes,
corals made of
pinks, silvers and metallic
greens.

The many years of edging knife,
what I call this earth's injury upon me.

I healed my wounds that day,
when I literally found heaven
in all the ocean life underneath.

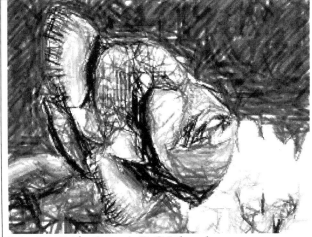

Marine Life Our A,B,C Islands

The Male Organ

The male organ was born from
a parasite on this large island shore.
Evolved over thousands of years
and numerous shapes.

Its head reared by the mere
fabric of earth.
A design some feverishly
argue was coincidental made
only from ape.

Host and predator,
its social behaviors,
in our ecosystems became,
naturally built.

The bringing up of light.
Transformed itself to the study of
human design.
Now these malformations
had to have been
aided from God.

Call it Awa, Hava or Eve,
angel, big bang theory
or miracle conception,
regardless in the end it
was one of its kind.

Parasitic is the highlight
what was called
the becoming better
of evolved?

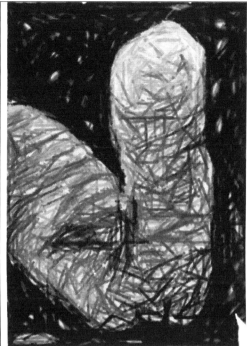

The Male Organ Redesigned A Parasite

A21- Australia

Amata

Child born were you from the womb
that was germinated from this soil.

Everything about you is made
from this black earth.

A22- Austria / Österreich

Earth's Keeper I am

The woman in me,
an extension of soil.
The early Amadeus of the
first songs of the ravens
that flew high.

Earth's keeper I am
locked in these mountains.
The view of the shaman
Hungry regions of Wachau's
landscape.

Our hands scabbed,
by the difficulties of land.

Our calves are a
mere trunk of a tree that
extends upwards
and waves freely in
the skies.

Earth's keeper I am.
Still existing in spirit.

Connect us as one soul today.

The Super organism Called Earth

The Elements of Fire

Long ago, life was really
hard for our first humans.
Hell was earth.

Scorn with hate many were for
all the suffering in place,
they endured.
Walked barefoot we did.
How the clusters of bare feet
transformed itself to hardened
orangey calluses.

Omens from our past found
deep, in Azikh's cave.
Nightmares from the
spawns of depth.
The sacred bones of our past
neatly buried.

Amplified were the pain
of our lives.
Some days, feelings of our
Internal, being burnt alive.
Some basics just didn't last.

Others will always remain
the incorporated emotions of
first people of earth,
who used the first elements
as controlled fire.

Fire

-B-

Baby Blue Crystal Glass

Baby blue are the waters
from the hilltop we can
see right through
the ocean floor.

Another one lost
say a group of Lukayan.
All we see are the tips
that glide through.

Emotionless they stand
still,
to watch the diving pelikans
eat the remaining remains.

The voices of fear,
we can still feel through
the breeze.
We ask the skies,
please can you just
leave us alone.

Give us some food they wailed,
and let these evil spirts
of land and sea
be gone.

Emblem Bahamas

Meaningful Female

Everything living in the
past had a story.
To our meaningful mother;
on the shore they went.
The region for centuries
known as Manama.
Tell us more, the heat
from the bonfire would soar.

We decorate the shores
for you.
We put tinsel and shells
we even put food and our
ancestry for you.

We light up the skies
with sacred fire.
Through the crackling of blaze
we pray for the many
of you in the skies.

Through the haze and hours of
circular chants a voice whispers
back to all of them.
Did you hear the one
about the stars
and how each one
represents our forefathers?
The biggest one being is Inanna.

She shines every night,
and slides across the heavens.
When people really believe in her.
Whisper her name seven times
and look high up. She will move again for
you. She is the mother that protects
all of your history.

The better place where your forefathers
go, after this planet discomforts you.

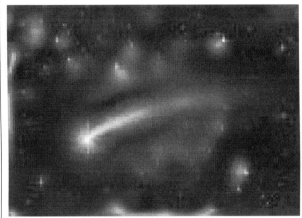

Shooting Star Of Inanna

Bengal Tiger

I am great it roared,
the noise rocked even earth.

The mushy waters lining up
Sundarbans mangrove forests.
Where it was happy in its
green tropical home.

No different than these
upright humans,
Gan Chi, the spirit of blood
in my region is exactly
what I am looking for.

A meal to make me stay
very still, for a few days
or more.

A silent predator, I am.
The arrow and bow
are my fierce claws.
The hunt, the life is the only
existence I surely know.

Bengal Tiger by Ganges

The Little Boy And His Bridge

Stories are what teaches,
this one is no different.
This is a tale of a little boy
and his favourite hangout bridge.

One day a truck was crossing,
and couldn't go under the low cover.
Engineers came so quick,
and try to solve this hover.

Confused were many.
More men came in.
We are going to have to tear it
down, this is how we will begin.

The little boy said, *please stoop*
can you simply think again!
Fixing can happen, just look at it
from within.

A bridge is a bridge,
don't tear it down please.
This truck is rare and filled
to the brim.
Making it an unusual crease.
Deflate its tires and they
can cross without being grim.

All men that day
realized something daunting.
When it comes to learning
you can see the light from any.

Bridgetown, Bridgetown Bridge Barbados

The Beloved Moon

We think of Europe so
cultivated and advanced.
Once upon a time
they too believed in the forests,
moons and chants.

Bialowieza primeval forest,
how you stand rare
and untouched.
The few left original landscapes
of Europe, what a work
of art by God.

Bison, otter, lynx still litter the
scene.

They tiptoe through the mist and
moved the pine trees to see the
bright moon in between.

The footsteps of human
ancestry when Europe
was green to the spleen.

And spirits made up souls
of the departed, when the
world just needed food.
The cleanest of the clean.

European Bison in Belovezhskaya- Pushcha
Forests

How God's Tears Made The Rivers

Blindness fills the people who live
between these shores.

We always feel their spirits.
Koksijde is our shamanic
territorial name.
Our first rest, before man
ever settled.

A different native we are, then those
who try to take our home.

Along the channels we fish,
but the heavens the sky
keeps pouring tears.

So upset the Gods must be.
Their noise and pounding has even
broken all the trees.

Even the land animals run clear.
The deer, the elk, foxes and eagles, the
bears have all gone inland.

We will follow them too.
But we promise spirits when we feel a
little warmth, we will come back
to the region we know as you.

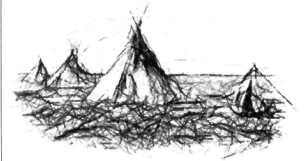

Koksijde Is Our Shamanic Name

Dear Spirits

I can hear you rustle through the wind?
As I walk they flutter all around me.
The sea salt touching my lips

A sense of mystery and magic.
I talk to them.

I was made in the mountains,
but I want to be buried near this sea.
My soul will connect to the spirits
and my flesh will finally be broken
from earth and mould with thee.

Our forefather's voices respond back:

Soil, the living, the life,
the feel of salt water on
your lips.
We are all around you.
Just close your eyes and
feel us.

Eventually you will connect
with us.
This is how the human flesh
merges with the skies.

You are the living, and your
surroundings has become
a homage to God.

That will finally set you free.

The Wind And Spirits

Sprits Of Africa

We were born here,
and make up
the 12 kings of rule.
We even sold slaves
to Europe.
Rich were we.

Until ships came to
the river of death,
to collect even the
fearsome
for voyage.

In Fon dialect
We said:
"You must be mad"
Royal is the palace
we live in.

Powerful commercial empire
we have!

White man are you that confused,
respect is what we demand?

The Tribal Kings Of Aborney

Clean Spirited Soul

Oh little bird why do you not fear me?
Sit on my hand.
Connect our spirits with this land.
I am stunned by your courage.

If a handful is that strong,
I am ashamed of my own song.
Little bird why do you not fear me?

Oh little chipmunk are you not scared of
me?
Hop in my tote.
I laugh at God's holy joke.
I play with your fur made up of an auburn
coat.
I am actually proud of your littlest
thunder.

If a tiny has might,
I should continue the flight.
Little chipmunk why are you not scared of
me?

Oh box size coyote you are so close.
Are you not afraid of humans,
your enemies of materialistic growth?

Touch my leg, with affection.
I can't help but wonder if you could talk.
How some of us would then be able to
save all your numbers?

If your little heart brings you this close.
I should copy your power.
Be like you, stand tall and be a great
tower.

Oh little coyote run away now,
if you stay still you will only be bailed away
by those who are your most destructive
force.

Animals always come to those with the
cleanest spirits and divine source.

Lamaistic Buddhism We Practice

The Landing Point, Tiwanaku!

We pray for every step
we carry our dead up.
Newly washed in God's holy
stream.
Gently rip the arms and the legs,
followed by the torso.
To create the smell of darkness.

They have started hovering
above us.
How they know our tribes
so well.
Another one
we screech and chuckle
back to them.

Grains we put in the wounds
we just made.
Take them to the moon,
make sure they come back.

Eat the flesh.
We will collect the bones
shortly and bury them in our
sacred sites.

This was our earliest mausoleum
in sending off our dead.

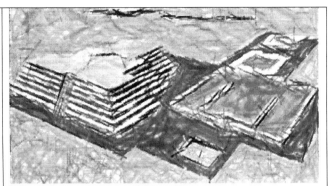

The Mausoleum of Death

Mehmet Pasha

I stand alone on this bridge its 1577.
I can feel the wind carrying the past
right through me.
The Drina river where the shamans
use to pray and wash their dead.
How violent could they have been.

I ask "how lucky I am to belong
to Ottoman territory".
This civil engineered and masterpiece
we just designed.
Will represent the future,
of a powerful and honourable colony.

Tell me the future is bright?
There is hope for tomorrow.
A tear I quietly shed for our ancestral
dead,
our animalistic believing God heads.

The red roses thrown today, off this bridge
is a reminder of our continuous struggle
as humans.

In the 21st Century with so much
technology.
A remembrance and prayer of those we
lose,
and continue to violently lose every day.

Sokolovic Bridge in Visegrad

Running Free With The Herd

The hostile land around Kalahari
is my home.

Many stories we tell.
These are our cuneiform written.
Forgive us we were the first on land,
this is all we knew.
A constant of habitat.
A battle designed between land and
hell.

Pictograms we would draw.
Songs we would sing.
Here is one for all.

> *Chase the antelope*
> *We run*
> *Be chased by the lion*
> *We run again*
> *A sweeping Sky God*
> *claws the back*
> *We all run!*

Who is the real king now we tell all
the men?

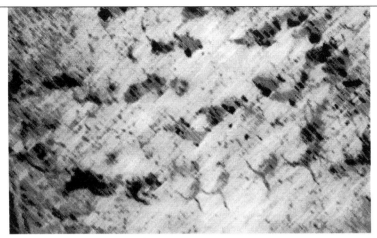

The Running Herd

Pink River Dolphin

Boto we would say,
your pinky colour just
blends in beautifully
with this tropical
landscape.

It is because of you we
feel to colour our houses
in full array.
How you talk and
play with us.

When we come to this
river basin
all we ask is a bucket
of fresh water.
An abundance that wont
bother your
way.

Pink river dolphin see
you again.
Tomorrow will be
another day.

Brazil's Pink River Dolphin

Sultanate

It's the 13th century, Hindu
is our beliefs declined has
become our Javanese Majapahit
Kingdom on our land.

The Sultan has ordered the
conversion of several
different tribes in the interior
to Islam.

They are still animists he says.

The caravans from holy lands
have reach India.
And trade is making us see
the light of the better Prophet.

The glamourous mosque,
the capital will now become
our very historic

Bandar Seri Begawan.

The Sultanate's Home, The biggest Palace
In the World

God's Gift

I was born gypsy,
God's gift is my name.

A blonde amongst all
the dark haired people
I live with.

Heaven's hotel is my musical
and humble home.

My whole life has passed here.

Amongst all the sadness,
all are people only ask
from God is as follows:

> *A little passion*
> *A little money*
> *A little clothing*
> *A little sadness*
> *A little love*
> *A little dance*

You have to find me, to see me.
The rich are no different, really.

This is how God tells us to be.

How our spirits should be,
These are his beliefs if he
exists somewhere.

We are his proud gypsies.

Heaven's Hotel

Find the spirits of the mountains our shamans once use to say…

The Spirits Of The Mountains

A World Once Before

Was it because of age, or how species use the land.
Before the deserts and the brittle soil.
Before the slave export and the grisly toll.

Africa was once glamourous.

The trans Saharan gold trade connected the ruins of Loropeni to many other points.

Ottomans thrive in where they were first linguistically born.

When trees relished in the horizon and birds sung in the breeze.

When tribes decorated their Kings and Queens, and relished them proudly in their homes.

When gold and many jewelries were made and plentiful in that zone.

The land whispered to us its once allure.
The oracle of written bones now deeply grinded, broken and lifted up by sand storm,
zone per zone.

Africa how you struggle today,
what went horribly wrong?

The little green's fight for survive on brittle lands.

The Mountains

Bujumbura we dance.
The tam tam of leather hide
drums.
The mighty spirits call us.

We are proud of the shamanic
mountains.
Some of our tribes call Burun.

Ut'ana the wild bird from the sky
who screams.

Indigenous and wild are our
spirits are.
Bujumbura we dance.

Our ancestral native scene.

Bujumbura Dance

-C-

Angkor

Flash of darkness
and blindness that daunts
our earliest.

We yell *"the blue skies are*
watching".
We need to erect immediately.

Human creative genius
when no influences existed.
An interchange of values.
Of those who process ancient
cultural traditions and hymns.

What part did Angkor Wat play
in humanities history?
Its beauty of rustic visuals and its
past.
The role of the burning in the
temple that was surrounded by
what was once holiest of water.

The eventual result became
a frontier of the highest
in early spirituality.

How an ancient world transformed itself,
into the dimensions of artistic horizons
and
higher consciousness.
What is now integrated oriental art
with that of the beliefs of shamanic first.

A beauty of eerie yet daunting
architecture;
and the spirits we can still feel that once
roamed its stone cold halls.

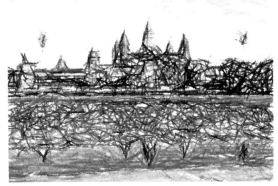

Angkor Wat Temple

Wah-za National Park

Deep in the jungle you will find the spirits that made humanity first start talking.

The watery Wah-za Park

C3- Canada / Kanata

The patriotic heart is made from the spirits of our past of those who have suffered
on the hardship of this lands. This applies to all, but it is

Our Natives we will proudly honour today.

Canada's New Skyline

Native we all are,
we really did not know.
Out came the voice of a past spirit
and now we are told.

Africa they were born.
Centuries later the Silk road
became their second
commute back home.

Tiptoed they eventually crossed
this treacherous Beringa road.

Loyalist made us proud Canadians
and unique like no others before.

A mix of many other countries later,
we nestled in big grey cities,
we call this our home.
But ill started becoming our souls.

We now run to our elders
and say, how can we make
new Canada's skyline?

Using our forefather's ancient
sensory and earthly goals.

Toronto Skyline

I Stole The Apple From The Bee

On the floor was a juicy red
apple,
fallen at the base of our
family tree.

Just when I was about to
grab it there on its other
side was a suckling bee.

Slowly I waved my hand
for him to fly away.
Go safely home to
your Queen.

And from my heart, I muttered
"sorry Mr. Bee,
but I just took this one
for us to eat".

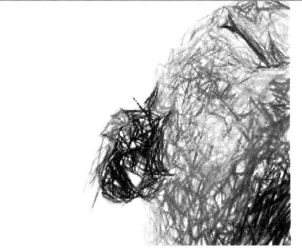

Suckling Bee

Shaman Was My Name

Two million years ago man got confused. He needed protection for the daily
tribal wars born from primitive behaviors of violence and abuse.

The term called distinctions was born,
a need to separate.
Centuries later, sealed became language.
What was known as the earliest vocal or sound range in the ululation alert of another clan's bait.

People suffered so much, depression hit more than once. The switch to feudalism transformed the role of money as a form of protective insurance.

The religious institutions became the first aid and everything prior that once existed became a massive illusion. The underworld then whispered to me.

Hidden in storages worldwide each countries records may be dusty and stored.
The narration of first vocals, our shamanic past, the shame of two thousand years of not knowing how to bring out their chronicles. This is the dishonor of our very own war-riddled ancestral past?

I pleaded, have mercy on humanities soul!

Make them release this immediately we are too advance! Are you trying to settle some type of warped psychological and hurtful score?

These community-based institutions still need a lot help today, let's never forget their primary role. To help aide the public and restore.
But gone are forced style collections, humans can still donate to be divinely bold.

This is not the story of a diamond and a coal.

Are we not democratic don't turn this into a nightmare called the academic brawl? How about if we go slower and work globally to bring forth.

Starting with our very own home base.
May every year on Canada's birthday,
one country releases something new.

Come on world, share these records!
Our shamanic goodies of our forefather's drawings or written, of their struggles and woes.

One At A Time

The Bering Confusion

"We are livid" they quietly said.
We are a multicultural country,
we have encountered a problem.
Blankly they quietly, asked each other:
Are first clans of earth, Asians?
How can they be if these descriptive
are a form of proto- Turkic from the many
regions?

Are first clans of earth black? How can they be
if there is a standardization about them and
they were found globally? Color is
predominantly climatically based?
She is right, but why didn't we think of that?

Could Natives just be Chinese now?
But they have phonetics even
belonging to Europe, and Africa?
First clans are Turkish?
That is what they are now all saying
Canada is ruined they fumed!

We are all Turks? We are so damn confuse!
We can't be link to them. The Natives are now
rattled! Who release this information?
Oh how they privately fumed?

God in this church I pray to you, injured is my soul, lost is my dominant arm, bored with tears I am. Many days and nights at home alone I read my hobby work to you. My papa teaches me Ottoman too. Then in the middle of the night, like a lightening strike that came bolting down.

A flash I saw. A glimpse of our unified human past. Hot water came boiling down.

Helplessness was the birth of the story that developed. Frantic to those who protect I ran?
Do you not understand social development; do you wish to ruin culture?
Even our Natives are not shaman but a distinctive culture.

You are the highest of the light?
Release this information immediately I yelled.
Callous nights of house arrest, genetic tests, it all violently began. Call it the "Bering strait Confusion".

The voices of distress is what I heard.
I am true Canadian, protect our blessed country, and culture! From those who break the rule of legal hand.

Horrid grief my bones are feeling now.
Figure out something quick, this was the hiccup of work, the gluing of hobby work in my many nights of loneliness that shadowed my pen.

Kanata, Ottoman Linguistic Analysis
Radicalization of language
Social Culture
The first 9 females who crossed
Use Of Technology
Pictionary Descriptive
What are First Clans
What are hominid phonetics
Standardization of what is a Shaman
Study of Populations, DNA
Color Saturation
What is Time
Topographical adjustments to Environment
Impacts of Political History
Logic of Slavery to World Wars
Migratory words
Self preservation
Natural Resources Study
Social behaviors
Defining Human, Human Territories
Religion of Birds
Two Million Years of Dialogues
Anatolian vs. Native
The fight for Africa
Who was the first Man
The conveyer belt theory etc.
Radicalization of Language
Defining Human
Progressive environmentalism
Constant Of Habitat

Turkish Girl

Who are you to tell us our own Native history?

Native chief don't you know,
I am an immigrant's daughter,
whose family tribe Alashan was
from the other side.
Gansu was its closest territory.
I just look different from thee.

Turkish Girl
You are wrong in your descriptive
of words, we know better than you.

Native chief don't you know,
Of the 9 or so females who crossed,
my ancient heritage is part of your heritage
and was also destroyed
in the process of being free.

Ever heard of the Ottoman toss?
Shamanic words of first it contained,
followed by an outmaneuver and the war of
Gallopoli.
Born was I on that land.
This I acknowledge is closer to me!

Turkish Girl
You will never be one of us.
We only support our tribes, the bands
that are made up of all the First Nation's people.

Native chief,
with all due respect.
Here is the difference
between you and me.
You came from the skies
and I was made in the
mountains and trees.
I am a human and this will forever now be

our connected ancestral tree.
I apologize if you look different from me.

I can assure I just understand some of your
inherited words of the first females,
that cross the Bering sea.

The birth of political linguistics

White Negro Child

I came to Canada as an immigrant's daughter in a very poor area of east end Montreal.

My father had purchased a 10 unit apartment building from Holocaust survivors, known as the Middlemen family. Who at 90 cried when their children removed them because of their age.

The day of departing Mrs. Middleman shows us her tattoo marked frail wrists and a suitcase non touched for years, of her hat and button collection. A reminder left to us of her working in the slums of a hat factory during Nazi occupation.

This particular building was close to the oldest apartment in the area by the railways.
Which interestingly held an entire building of the first Asian migrants and built not at city code but more petit in standards. A building entirely designed at that time to their general size.

The area changed over continuously. Each era bringing in new immigrants from a diversity of backgrounds.
By the time we had really settled an influx of West Indies had immigrated and had taken smaller size apartments in the area.

The weight of managing a building alone took a horrid toll on my dad who now became an absentee parent. My mother on the other hand completely new even in communication became isolated and developed mental despair.

Corn braided was my adopted mother. The inside of her palms unlike others, was a beautiful light ebony black representing one part of her interesting Amerindian background. A trait left only to a very few indigenous remaining in her parish.

Child she would say for a white girl you have thick curly blonde hair; you must have black in you. Growing up with them, I would yell back don't you dare call me white. Confused horribly at my own identity mixed in with them for years.

Her own daughter and I had made a pack to be blood sisters for life. Our community of island people was comprised of a school that had a black female principal and black teachers. An attempt by Canada to make comfortable its influx of island immigrants.

The Black Community Center that we would go to housed the oldest center in Canada to improve life after slavery was abolished. Established by Jewish and black female women, trail blazers they were named, for attempting to push progress.

Today as we look at the beauty and variety of the multicultural families across North America. A new bond of integration and tolerance is forming. Merged with the development of my own historical timeline, and the research presented to University of Toronto to demonstrate the irregularities of defining humans in the light of academia of past.

We can justly mark this as monumental defeat towards evolving, humanities push in civil and human rights in the 21st Century.

I can honestly say I am very proud, I was raised as a white negro child today…

C'est La Vie

Non, rien de rien,
non, je ne regrette rien!
Ni le bien, qu'on m'a fait
Ni le mal; tout ca m'est bien égal.

Pour nous
C'est toujour c'est la vie
Aujourd'hui, hier et à l'avenir
nous ne regrette rien!

Vieux Montreal

What Has The Blues Given?

What has the skies given to us in terms of defining humans as superior beings?

The heavens simply taught us tolerance.

The act of loving all the imperfections, cultural variant, physical and topographical related traits God has created here on earth.

What Has The Greens Given?

What has the land given to us in terms of making human.

The heavens simply taught us where our souls and history germinated from.

That the dirt on the ground has to be felt, and touched, made respected.
Our connection to protecting earth is part of all our ancestry

The Blues And Greens Of Earth

The Isles Off Africa

Christopher Columbus said,
"What beauty are these islands
off the shores of Africa.

Our stop is temporary, the pillories
all across the island
upsets my soul too much.

Plus, this area is secure the new world
allows us to explore a lot more for our
country."

Christopher Columbus Visual of a Slave in a Pillory

Chari River

They have come. Be careful child.
Call it the devil in disguise.
Deep into the marshlands they went;
slavery decimated its original
indigenous.

But by the hopeless river,
take a second and study
the channeling flow of breeze.
And its gushing swell.
That once carried water
to the many parts of the Gaoga
 empire.

Animals, the French had yelled.
They wear vibrant feathers
and run half naked amongst the low
plateau
of savannah.

They do look graceful though we must
acknowledge.
Blended in spirits, when they kill not
a single animal runs.

Our guns strike many down.
Empty we will make their land.
In one hundred years' other tribes
will move in.

We will continue slavery till no end.

Running Free

The Shamanic Prayer

Sing praise
Sing praise
To the terrapins
linked to the skies.

The moon glistening and
translucent in nature.
Vibrant is the mist surrounding our Shan.
Smokey with the dust they spew,
lifting our spirits.

Sing praise
Sing praise
To this food given,
protect us.
We do this for you,
oh Josh-hua.

We dance,
around the fire.
Circular in format.

Hide our faces with earth
materials blessed from
the clouds that hover.
Sing praise
Sing praise

May our souls be heard.
The first tamgas of earliest life,
the skies have given us.
We dance for you.

Prayers From The Skies

The Stans Of Central Asia

Kazak
Krygz
Other tribes within Russia
Tajik
Turkmen
Uzbek

We our what is called in Farsi the place
of the standing people, the Stans.
Our tribes are all different.

Centuries prior we would continuously
battle each other.

Today we just tell the world we don't need
to, our borders were created
to separate one another.

Our flags tell the world the differences
in each other.

The Different Indigenous Of Turkic Countries

Quilted Tapestry

Your prehistoric Neolithic sites
scattered throughout.
A quilt woven of
over 100 different languages
and dialects.

A rich world not known.
Of opulent literature representing
the creations of first life.
Millions of years of verbal history
and picturesque rock art.

Kingdom of Kanem.

Ignorant man be for not understanding
the tribes of Sara, Tangule and Buduma
To name a few of the many.

Your black-blue skin of beauty
that once had traversed.
And had linked your tribes making
up territory from the equator line to the base
of the Mediterranean Sea.

Your quilt centuries long
represent one of our most ancient
starts of humanity.

Chad Tribesman

The Black Mummy

We are the ancient ancestry to the
Picunche people;
we have just invaded another tribe.

The women are ours.
The men and children we kill.

The children we feel somewhat
remorse.
So we collectively pick
a few and put pelican skin
on their faces.

As our youth prepare them for
the afterworld.
We eat some of the body parts,
urinate on them
so they don't return to kill our own.

We cut our own hair and pick the
adolescence in the tribe who
have seen 10 winters to put it
on these new mummies.

We are attempting to desecrate
our enemies' ancestry.

This is called our ritual of manhood,
where our youth have to stuff them
with earth, and cover the empty
body cavities with ash paste.

Our youth have now become men
and will learn to hunt some more.

Once the mummification process
has finished we will dance, so sure
their spirits will not be an omen, our
spiritual prance.

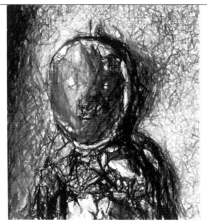

The 5,000-Year-Old Black Mummy

Cave Person

Cave person can you hide
anymore?
You walk half up right and down,
oscillating left to right.

You eat raw meat.
Yet you fear like the many
other animals before you.

Cave person
When did you become human
is not the key?
Barefoot and torn were all
your feet.

You started with a few words,
and the utilization of
tools in your bag of hide.

God put his hand on your
shoulders one day.
Made you permanently
stand upright.

He went on and sent angels
from the heavens above.
That alleged:

Help them educate
the divine way,
the holy book will be sent
and made in gold from the skies.

Cave person something
magical is happening now.
We can reveal your history
accurately and not be bound
by the historic reason's of
hidden by God.

Standing Upright

C19- China

Dark Fairy Mountains

Our altar to heaven
were the mountains.
The magnificent seven
were they tip by tip.

They were called
Peri-shan.
To eat means the holy
shamanic seven.
One more ate, after eight.

Ustra did they bring.
The dark fairy mountains.

Cultures of devastation.
Our shamans,
brought them food.
Sprits of destruction
became our
dark fairy mountains.

Dark Fairy Mountains, China Seven Points

C20- China

He (ké.key) is the name of the flowing
river.

Hé

Your Majesty,

Our people have so
much honour.
We too are Royal.
Ornamented we brand
them in red.

We were the first real
humans, refined was our style.
Why do you hide
thee?

We had pyramids
before others,
we had written
before others.

We also migrated
to Africa,
thousands of years
prior and integrated.

We produced gun powder,
astronomy, nautical and macaroni
noodles to the world.

Our battles were fierce.
Mongoloid labelled, were
we back then.
That others claimed all of
these historically.

Ignorant be not!
Your own people, your heritage.
Part of Europe's ancestry,
is also linked to us.

Why do you hide thee?

Little Emperor

Blue Eyes

In southern Turkey
elders would say,
blondes were our first.
Blues we were meant to stay.

Overtime our clans grew.
Discrimination we did not.
What is a human, we knew
back then.
Interestingly from Egypt, to Algeria
all got thrown in our evolutionary pot.

A few humiliations and defeats,
our trails became too wide.
Lively-hood in pace,
growth was still our pride.

Transitions from one point
to a next,
conquering became our
trade.

Kiev became our second
home.
Never once did we betray.
Time went by, the depth of
intermix became our bay.

Elders in southern Turkey now say,
hazel eyes were our second,
beautiful light browns we were
meant to stay.

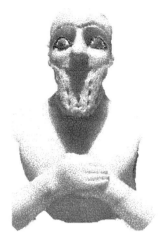

Our First Blues

By The Railway

On the railway to Popayan,
we arrive at an ancient kingdom of 1889
called Armenia.

There the name resemblance echoes.

A prayer is told:

Greater is he than that which is in you,
out of suffering the emergence of
strongest souls behold.

Be still and let the lord judge
the wrongs of those that once
were uncontrolled.

The guidance and gift of
higher force,
we thank your power
O'Lord.

Amen

Prayer To Heal

The Essence Of Vanilla

The rain sinks so
deeply into the lava,
that the porous rocks
of Grande Comore turns
the water to brackish.

Yet through the hard
conditions of land the
vanilla oils
for export are still
provided to the world.

Mount Kartala,
before the haven of pirates or
man became permanent.
Before James Lancaster ship arrived
in 1591.

Do you remember?

The tropical climate,
the hand tied twig floats
to cross.
The bare and injured feet of the many
that hid on the islands
for centuries.
The beauty of land, birds and lemure.

The influx of African mainlanders of
mixed diversity which became the start
of our permanents.

A story of life, way before Jumhuriyat
became us in 17th Century.
Our people a mix race making up
Africans, Arabs, Indonesians
and Iranians.

Who like our ancestry, just enjoyed
the wind and the salty air.

Bird In The Wind

Congo's Genocide

For each era that has come and
gone, violence has consumed us.
Middle Africa.
Not 1, 2, 3 or 4, more, like 5
million or more.

All painfully brought to earth,
with love and care.
Evil became the rage of the lifeless
bodies who were mutilated and sent
back.
The catalyst of what is horrific warfare.

Not a single remembrance globally
for future children to shed a tear.
Lower than our animal instinct,
the value of no human worth.

The truth is the dynamics of pressurized
soils became the tragedy of what
was to be unearthed.
Pain beyond belief.

The heaven's now proclaimed:

> *Always give a hand*
> *to those in need.*
> *Communicate for civility and*
> *will find forever find relief.*

> *Put seeds of bloom,*
> *as remembrance for the*
> *decease.*
> *Make this tragedy of souls,*
> *never ever bleed.*

Keep the memory of these deaths active,
its analysis in the future is what will
keep humanity alive one day.
The vision of what is less drastic.

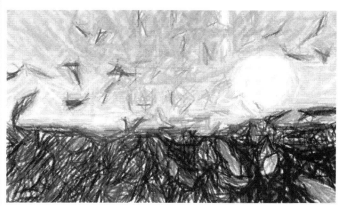

Flowers In The Breeze

Teke, The Minority Is This Tribe

Ku Ku Ku …

We the Kouyou!
Mimic we do the ones in the sky,
tribes with feathers and violent
we are not liked by the others.

The Italian-born French explorer
Pierre Savorgnan de Brazza
in 1875 made a treaty with
our people the Teke.
That made our Kingdom under
French protection.

We now became a different
game of delight.

Ku Ku Ku…

We were never liked.

Ku, ku, ku we call the ones in the sky

Tropical Nights

The indigenous desire in me,
they said we have none but
I ignore.

I feel that I want you,
that I need you.
Sorry for melting in your arms.
You are my life and spirit,
you are in my mind.

Every time I see you I feel
beautiful things.
Desire, oh desire carry my
lighted torch.
Give me the chance to be on
your side,
if you leave I will never
forget you come to me.

You give me the strength
to continue.
Tropical flowers make up
your scent,
the silk of your hair,
the touch of your skin.

Its desire, oh desire.

Continuing burning in me like a flame.

Tropical Nights

Pygmy Hippopotamus

Shaman youth
we are together for a long
time in this tree.

When I screamed for you
to climb,
I pray to the ones flying,
you followed me.

You see that thing in the
water, it is watching us.
These ones are smaller in size.
This does not matter.

When you come close to
the bank and lay down
on the ground to drink.

Once you see those ears flop
side to side.
Run like a lion was chasing
you and forget any of your pride.

Run Shaman Youth

Wild Horse

Wild horse are you tamable?
Wild horse find the other
two hundred that have left you.
Roam do you do, so iconic
in nature.

The biggest colt of them all.
Near Livno the plains of heaven
your fields way beyond yonder.
Rugged you climb Cincar,
your spirit wild and free.

Wild horse
Will you submit to us?
Farmland is way too many acres,
hands we would need to help feed?

The souls of those who once
try to grasp you still can be
felt in the nightly breeze.

Wild horse
Please be free!
Run wild your background land,
has become the colors' of Duman.
The smoky grey streams,
the rugged stones under your hooves.

Makes us watch your precious beauty.
and know there had to have been a
creator
that was beyond artistic belief.

Coldblood Horses Croatia

Oh How I Love The Cuban People

Their beautiful brown skin, and mix of
Spanish Afro style beats.
Their humbleness to God, and being
human.
The safest of all the islands.

Oh how I love the Cuban people.
Their old American landscapes and cars
dates back to the 60's.
They would sing to me their version of
love to the skies above.

Guantanamera

I am just a truthful man from the land of
the palm trees before I die I want to share
my poems from my soul.

> *My poems are soft green.*
> *My poems are also flaming crimson.*
> *My verses are like a wounded fawn*
> *seeking refuge in a forest.*

Guantanamera

My words are spoken sincerely,
and rings in with hopes for tomorrow.
I speak of life and its promise,
I know its joys and its sorrows.
The streams of the mountains
please me more than the seas.

Guantanamera

I always say I choose the poor as my
people and share their dreams and their
troubles.

"The prayers of God are what we all look
for."

Love For The Skies

Run My Loved Ones

The war is here, villages
they are plundering and burning.
Our people are so human.
They have been casted an evil
spell.

Mother and her three young children,
have run far from their homes.
Where the father awaits
to divert the enemy.
You may be able to save yourselves he
whispers to her.

> *I am praying to you so deeply,*
> *the heavens above.*
> *Beads of prayers in one hand, the dull*
> *kitchen knife awkwardly in another.*
> *My faith has finished here.*
> *Protect my family he glares.*

A sniper pierces through
his body.

> *Split second of memories*
> *flash by.*
> *Years of love making,*
> *His children, holding hands.*
> *The land of grapes hanging.*

His other half on the hill top watching
the body flung around by the
darkness of foreign, now wails.

In the distance hearing the chimes of
Ayia Sotira.

The Tears Of Remembrance

Christ's Halo

The poor begged for his life,
Tar o, lay low
Tar o, lay low
They quietly wail.

Don't eat God's chosen one,
on this old rickety wood cross.

Ku ku ku,
The punishers call on the skies with
anger as they set him up.

Take
Al – in, nan,na
Al – in, nan,na
They scream in retribution.

Those around him were very poor
yet they ran and sacrificed
a deathly thin animal, close by.
Hopeful the ones in the sky will
stay busy.

While we bring him
down, after dark.
Tar oh please- lay low
Tar oh please- lay low

Dark clouds over us,
we beg the skies for mercy on our
chosen's life.

His purity and halo blessed.
We kiss his feet.
Please fight for your life.
Cries,
It doesn't work.
The smell of blood,
quickly attracts the many spirits of
Tar, in the skies.

Watch Them, We Say.. Eat You Alive

-D-

The Cultural Touch

The journey across Scandinavia,
one of the strongest holds.
Its Gothic cities and landmark heritages,
couldn't digest what was being told.

I had to be clever and real fast, if I was not I
would definitely not last.

> Denmark is the center of civility and
> law, is what they barked, it has been
> this way for years this is the only way
> we know how.

> We have many things completely
> distinct to us, including the oldest
> welfare system and benefits if you
> must.

> In addition, might we say,
> beyond human we are, a Christian
> God's perfect development, this has
> always been our only way.

But there is another side to this I presented.
Don't be surprised now that Denmark has
relented.

I said don't get confused with the picturesque
marks of earth a lot of us all see.
Like tectonic plates stacked
one on top of another,
the first words of life, are the emergence
of our very own ancestry.

The dark to light, like a spectrum of colours.
These were simply blended in glee with
animal howls of first others.
Jutland became an example
a form of singing in the breeze.

From Denmark to China back then took
only two years for the migration to flee.
Disorderly is humanities first dialogues in
what is call our earliest jubilee.

Denmark

Understand what is to Evolve and it will make
you see, why dialogues became one of our
ugliest political decrees.

The theme is now shamanic!
An attempt to convince with legal right.
Green is the path, the aura of our
ancestral lights.
Follow your indigenous past this will
be a different type of flight.

It is one part of how humanity will last,
something horribly missing from our historical
past.
Designation was your clan.
Cultural heritage back then became your
holiest fight.

The illustration became human
interconnectedness,
and what is now called the critical
cycle of life.
This is how humans will win, with
zero might.

The Nissum Fjord

The glaciers cut deep this particular Fjord.
Formed from glaciations millions of years old.

Its 100,000-year-old first settlements.
Whispers to us the spirits, of what was once told.
Each year that had gone, missed something, from a story so old.

Here is of how simple the land developed our first tasks. For this, we will now commemorate our shamanic past.

Our ancestry has become such a great honour. A calendar is an example of the visuals of what the land had to first offer.

At the start of equinox each year, the waters levels let us know that winter had elapsed.
And spring will allow us to bare.

Back then we knew no better than what our land the fjord, told. They became our only measuring point the marks of our ancestors, and their existence to live practically blindfold.

Babylon and Hebrew were linguistically no different in other zones.
It is the age of Europe's historical habitat that is the question of this linguistic loan.

The start of descriptive visuals if I must say, possibly thousands of years old began developing in the oddest of ways.

Nisan is Hebrew, while Nissum on the other hand was Europe's first in the same way.

But it was the Gods, their spirits, making holy their water called Tan-ni. The irony of it being from India, thousands of miles away. Makes this story slowly starts to unfold.

Which regional phonetic was really first we will never truly know?

Nissum Fjord

The Market In Djibouti

The Afar or Danakil people
have seen the Portuguese, Italian,
French and African traders.

The oldest caravan routes were linked
to their Abyssinian plateau.
Where you would find the Centre of
Djibouti city life.

There in the markets, centuries ago the
following
items were sold:

*Food, daggers, knives, necklaces of amber,
wooden objects, root dyed handmade outfits,
silk and silver jewelry.*

Today when we go to the market you
will find the following:

*Food, daggers, knives, necklaces of amber,
wooden objects, chemically dyed outfits, silk
and silver jewelry.*

Our Daggers

The Boiling Lake

This person is a witch an
omen from the sky Gods!
The Carib's once said.

Throw them into the boiling lake.
Watch their spirits melt
and never come back.

Smell the sulfur and flesh mix.
When the bones are left.
The dance of death we will do.

The Thermal Spring Called Boiling Lake

1844 War Of Independence

Please bless us and split our
island in two from the French
speaking dark skin Afrikana tribes that
conglomerate to the West of our island.

We are not like them, at all.
Our people are of mixed blood.
Hispaniola and Caribs, are to name a few.
But we even have German Jews in all of
this brew.
We are way too different culturally.

The split means we are finally protected
in our perspective territories.

We can now celebrate this grace of Victory.

Cultural Costumes- Dominicana

-E-

Almost Human

Man said we came
from ape.
Women said we are possibly
still ape!

Ecuador became the footsteps
of this researcher's holiest place.

Through dense jungle, Darwin's
path she wanted to follow.
In search of defining what is
human this time.

Forested indigenous,
barefoot you walk.
Wild is your look,
with eye-make up
so stalked.

Tell me if you have seen human?

Yes, we have:

> *They are here protecting*
> *the forests.*
> *Praying to the skies,*
> *And living in peace with the surroundings,*
> *around them.*

Forested indigenous,
have you ever heard of Darwinism from
possibly another researcher that may have
travelled along?

But more importantly how man was
derived?

No we have not can you explain he smiled:

> *They are here swallowing up everything,*
> *they are on earth even extinguishing*
> *forests.*
> *Believing we just showed up with no belief*
> *from the skies.*
> *They are destroying all their surroundings.*

Forested indigenous can you please pray for us.
Your humanist soul is what we need right now…

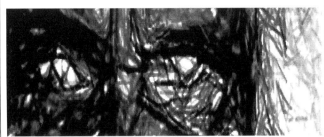

In Search Of Human, Shaman Man

The Spirit Of Tutankhamen

The Valley of Tombs.
A king's reign, vaulted in.
Opens so slowly.
Hieroglyphs now give us
such a story.

The son of Merit-Rā.
Glorified, the blessed soul of Africa's
Tan was he.
He was just one of the many.

A prior disposition to represent all of
the black charcoaled out-lined eyes,
of our shamanic past.

We call on you holy spirits in the sky.
We worship the heavens,
the many priests who had
aided his essence in the process.

Deity after deity,
We had prayed to the heavens.
The tower of pyramids,
our made to honor the many who had
passed by.

Wings had once adorned our sphinx,
history removed them satanically.
Little is known on our real history.

In the essence of life today we
are attempting to do such a recovery.

May Aten finally rest.
The slow conversion to Egypt's
monotheistic beliefs, cultural development
and our own progress at its very best.

The Spirit Of Tutankhamen Lives

The Warrior Known As Musa

Before the Red sea parted,
before any exodus,
before Canaan was taken
over.
Or the Pharaohs in Egypt.

Their existed a Moses
but his shamanic name
was Musa.

From Persia,
he came blaringly defiant to survive.
Migratory were his clans,
with very large stallions.

His team was strong as hell.
They destroyed everything
in their paths.

Centuries later,
holding an infant out
of the Nile's water.
A voice whispered.

> *"You too are a Musa.*
> *A word to mouth story*
> *of a warrior's*
> *past historical strengths,*
> *when no real written existed."*

But it was God that made the
most remarkable spell,
when it came to Prophet Moses.
He blessed earth for what is betterment.
The reason behind what God said to
Moses:

> *"Selected, I have deemed you now as having*
> *divine origins. For the ethical and moral*
> *teachings, of the ancestries of your clans".*

Remember what is human and these sacred scrolls.

Your people are Chosen humans, designed with no flaws.

Perfect in human intention.
You were design specifically from heaven.
Even before you were born.

Just fill your prophecy!
A transposition has taken place
and forget your shamanic divination,
for a new light has been born".

The Transition to Moses

Spectrum Of Light

We were born from a single
Bacterium that replicated
and carried the
photosensitise of light.

Migratory and crawler
became the living
as the tectonics of earth
changed their part.

Some formations became
spectacular
no different than art.
Corals, pinks, azure
and venetian reds
are just some of the
colors that gave way.

It designed all the
creatures of earth,
in the most sheerest
of delight.

When we look at colors
Let's understand all
the hues.

For all our vibrant forests
are merely a by product
of copied light.

We are thankful El Salvador
for the reforestation introduce
to increase our colorful lives.

The Colour Of Life

The Fang Chief Said:

If you and a fool dance,
you will win.

If you and a fool have
an argument, he will win.

If you and a fool make love,
You will both win.

As a chief, speak only to those
who are above you.

African Proverb

The Admiration Of Aksumite Empire

We were independent until we
fell under Ottoman rule.

We taught them what our
forefathers use to say.

That compassion was developed
from three words.
To see, feel and act.

What our earliest saw;
What they felt deep in their souls;
And their reactions to their outcomes.

Anyone acting immorally we would
let them bleed.

We are still part of this legacy.

Ak the symbol of spirits that are
flowing, called the white of death.

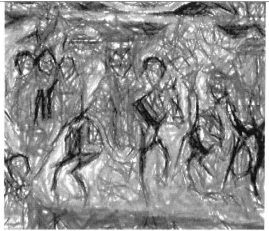

Aksum Region

The Transformation of Tallinn

Bipedal barely, our first humans
were screeching throughout Europe.
By the shore of Tallinn, they dragged
the bodies by the feet
to feed the sky Gods.

Epochs of slow light and
distorted time.
A flourishing town, gradually
developed into the Hanseatic
League.

Estonia's became a trading city.
With medieval times churches
and its castle that housed its
crusading knights.

Nowadays a remarkable urban
Fabric with European style
precise geometrical structural
forms.

Winding streets and fine
public burgher buildings.
Restored is St. Nicholas' Church.

This is the very slow transformation
of just one historic European city.

Heritage at its finest best.

Tallinn

Kingdom Of Kush

Earlier than Selassie,
Ethiopian born,
I ask you.

"Why do you adorn yourself,
with those colours,
of green, yellow and red"?

Child do you not know?
"These are part of our shamanic
rituals of past".

Red is the blood that our forefather's bled.
Yellow was the moon and sun
we prayed to.
And green was the religion of earth
before any man settled.

Earlier than the Solomon Dynasty,
we are the historical first civilizations
of Africa.

I understand this, but why then
do you follow the revolution
of stars?

Child do you not know?
"These are our shamanic
beliefs of the past".

The stars guide us to the
Kanat that flies.
Their beaks carry up,
our ancestry to the hungry Gods.

And our Kingdom of Kush is where
our territories began, way
before any man settled.

Flag of Ethiopia

The Moon Dance

Underneath the moon
we dance.
In complete darkness,
the sole light that exists.

The multitude of the lunar
faces, we study.
Our palms reach the skies.
We ask for what is in between
the moon and earth Mez-ayah,
we scream.

Our symbol for illumination,
and some warmth.

Many Gods hear our voices.
Protect us, we say.
From the curse of darkness that
doesn't fetch our ancestry back.

With the faint shimmer
of hope, all we ask from you is,
take our dance and mourning,
and bring these spirits back.

From The Skies To The Torah

Two Wild Horses

Put two wild horses
in an enclosure,
they will madly kick
around and even try to bite.

Watch their struggle,
in a web called the
unknown fury of life.

Even if one is bigger
and the smaller is getting
injured in the end the
horses know their destiny.

Its masters have locked them
together in a small holding area.
They gradually over time
get use to living with this
dominance of might.

This is called the analogy
of social behavior.
Helpless these two
horses are now
unified in a rut.

Both understand they
are destitute
and jailed in.
To the powers of a
master's vision
of humbling the
beauty of wildlife.

Humans are no different
and are also sealed
into earth's walls.
They too feel helpless
and locked in.

But this time the skies are
our master,
they are watching over us.
Humbling continuously
the beauty of
their wildlife.

Helpless early humans then
developed
the many Laws of life.

Do you now
understand how ethics and rules were born?
The power of humans to be civil in
earth's walls of life.

Dedicated To The Wild Horses Of Eurasia

The Birth Of Satan

Ruler of the dark,
the one evil that can control earth.
How did you come to be?

Your wings filled with might,
your mouth hovers over our dead.
Did we do you wrong that we mourn
today?

All we ask from you was the
noblest pleasures of earth be ours.
Contentment, we wish to pursue,
without the darkness that comes to us.

Oh spirits, talk to us.
Salvage us from this dark ruler of Tan.

Şey-"Tan"
        Say-"Tan"

The evolution of "Satan" has began.

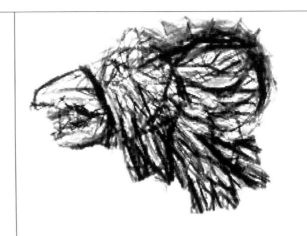

Say-Tan

The Group Of White Knights

White men adorned,
were our Vikings.
With shamanic head gear,
and steel armor.

Never once did we see
anything so fierce.
The family of druids were
their leads.
Around the henge,
into the uncharted.

Little clothes in the winter,
fearless in nature.
Wild in behavior became our
white ones with metal gear.

White Knight

The Private Race Of Man

When all men on earth once
came from different sources.
Animal we must still have been
for not seeing the light of
the work presented.

In a dark room locked in I am.
The role has flipped, as a researcher, I
actually study them.

A secret, my sensory
now picks ups.
Of a fierce battle in Geneva
that has began.

Of what was first race,
their dialogues and who was
actually first man.

Like blood in shark infested waters.
I watch social mock of each other.
The highlight of distinction
now broke them to a massive flutter.

I raised my hand and quietly said:
  When you accept and face humanity
  all of you will be able to advance today.

None of these arguments are important, if
you can just define to me what is

    "A Human?"
That landmass one was two million
years of a blended fusion that made
our earliest handful of shamans.
To that of a gradual saturated DNA
mix, human adaptations and a lot of
academic past confusions.

The uniqueness of God's creation was
centuries of saturating his hominids.
The colours, styles and shapes were
made because of the topography of
the many lands and their waters.

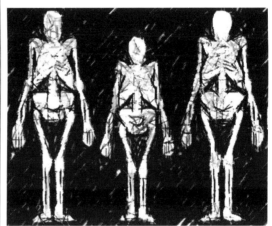

Define Human?

-F-

F1- Fiji   F2- Fiji

Paradise Cove	Kula Eco- Park
Well my friend, I like to eat, sleep, drink and be in love… Paradise is all I need!	We constantly sing in the mist of the night, but one thing I must say to you. If there was only one moon, I still would not share this beauty with you.

The Boy And His Lantern

My name is Hans Christian
he whispered.
I am so wet and it is cold
outside, please can you let me in?

It is spring and it still feels
midwinter.

Child which district are you from?
The man asks?

We live at the base of Haltaitunuri.
The war did so much damage,
and I have another 10km to go
before dawn.

> *The man's fire-light was dim,*
> *here take this he said.*
> *It's a small glass of wine and a*
> *roasted apple, please just stay warm.*

Hans continued, I have landmarked
the pine trees, this is the way I
reroute back home.

The peat bogs I keep slipping into,
the wax I carry is enough to bring
me home.

When the rain stops,
I will make my long journey back.
I really need to get home.

The Lantern in the Forest

Fontainebleau

Sitting nude
in the small vibrantly
clear blue creek.

Near a tap cracked opened
by the pressurized
mountain's vein,
my hair dangles.

I am life!
I touch my breast.
A uterus in floating water.

My leather shoes
hung on a low
tree limb.
To dry the scent
embedded on hide,
of earth mixed with
human sweat.

Made by God's
loving hand.
His child of
Grace.

Hoping the impact
of man,
doesn't rip my soul.

I ask the spirits
please but please
protect me.

From the surroundings
I live in and our earth's
dangerous tolls.

The Uterus In Floating Water

The Breaking Of Human Distinction

How dare you they barked,
we are not African or coming
from there!
What are you trying to say?

I said humbly

You may be right, or
you may be wrong.
Do the test called
the nipple size
and it will solve the
problem of your day.

Don't get offended with the
colors of first,
we all came from ape.
This is not a curse.

You need to change
how you think.
And our missing ancestral
link.

The moving DNA that once
roamed, our spirits of past
life to that, of what is a human
chromosome!

Let's forget everything for a
minute I say.
The focus is social betterment
and this should be humanities
new way....

Defining A Hominid Trait

Nuit Noir

Windings roads, cobble stone floors.
Tiny flowers each window still
carries high.

Hold a glass to the Eiffel tower;
Chardonnay, Pinot and Bordeaux.
Are the wines in aged display
in each corner store.

The life of a Parisian.
Historic and rich, full of lively core.
An opulent cultural mixed
with old and new.
Artistic all displays are,
in imminent form.

But have a look at their language
and let's not be in the dark,
anymore.

England had all the fun!
With hat, bat, cat and mat.
But it didn't finish there.
Many more existed all
in the simplest nursery-rhyme form.

The French language is perfection
in its altered state.
We can analyze these dialogues
further, can't you see the precision
of this grammatical state!

They brought out Bescherelle and
thousands of verbs,
all in enlighten form with complex
structural schematics.

To tell the world we were and still are
the highest academically.

The reason is simple. English is way older
if we attempt to put it chronologically.

Hittite started the base of phonetics from
the very start of their cuneiform tablets
found underneath.

France at the time was nowhere near,
this
developmental build.

The language known as romance,
came way later.
A design constructed very organized and
clear.

Eiffel Tower 1887

The Battle Beyond D-DAY

I walked into the historic
hall entrance of University of Toronto.
There on a plaque is a reminder,
of the boys no older than twenty
sent to war.

Cold brass has become tarnished,
forgotten with the stains
of tears over the years it has hung.
A list way long.
They fought for our freedom.
How fortunate we are;
as I attempt to see if I can dust one corner.

Thousands died on the beach in the
first five minutes.
Some yelled for their mothers.
The bullets were made in Germanized,
newly designed auto-format;
pierce through several times
their thinned out bodies.

Etched became their memories
on Omaha beach that day.
No different than their earliest
ancestor's battles for survival.
The blood soaked sands became just
another defeat, another reminder.

Today through understanding
and human consciousness,
a long journey our road has become.

One towards advancements.
We pray for their souls. We proudly shine
their plaque on the wall to remind us that
we are still in a fierce battle.
An enchanted gold gate, gardens
of birds and flowers. Living we want to
place back.
May their innocence or suffering be turned
into a bed of roses. Called *The Giving Back
Life To Those Who Died Violently.*

Majority of our people are mulatto,
like they love to say.

But our blacks speak Taki Taki,
and refuse to be address to downplay.

We don't like Mulatto

-G-

A Spoon Made From Food

We have some interesting dishes.
Our original inhabitants were in majority
Pygmy who consumed very little meat.

Our regions nowadays make up 40
different territories and languages.

They will eat a variety of food.
Antelope jerky, salted fish, fried bats
and roasted caterpillars to name a few.

However, in general our early morning
meals remain the same across Okano.

If you want a spoon for your
breakfast you will have to mold it from
the pressed grains we have provided
and then use this edible spoon to eat.

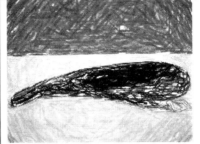

Spoon Made From Grains

By Gambia's River

When these European explorers first arrived in the 14th century they came to our very large Kingdoms.

We kindly showed them our woodcarvings, batik cloth printing, weaving gold and silver jewelry making.

Batik Method Of Dyeing

Why Are The God's Crying

Why are the skies releasing tears,
the darkness pounders light.
Fear runs through our shivering bodies.

Why are the God's crying?
During Paleolithic times we hid
in what was once called
the departing caves.

In the mountains we gradually
transformed these death dwellings
into Vardzia, our permanent home.

It was our only form of security
from invaders
who had avoided the caves of death
and "the Gods" in case they sent their
omen wings after us.

Mortified in thought we still prayed
for life.
The fear that another one, will not
come back?

Why are the God's crying? We wait
till the skies stop.

Zia, The Candle Light Of Death

Bird In The Wind

One by one they filled
Germany's ghettos.
All selectively picked,
another side to Schindler's list,
        One that never really unfolded.

Papers were scattered on my desk.
Night after night,
the dawning inclination that
there was more of Ottoman
then what was historically told.

The only way to understand them,
was to envision their strategic view.
To understand the mind
of what is called a radical pursue.

The war began,
symbolism they needed.
Something indigenous
taken from the land.
The running bird in the
wind now became their new
ugly force in command.

Machinery after machinery,
what a push for control.
Not a bullet was needed!
Advance and leave them
nude for five minutes in the
coldest of the cold.

Underground treaties,
Russia would have had to have
secretly opened doors.
What was Hitler really looking for,
only a select few will know.

Claiming Back The Indigenous Symbol

Aachen Cathedral

The prophecy from the skies said
"Be aware!"
From its inception the screams of
past can be heard.

The torment and torture to convert.
The painful transition that had to have
existed on earth.
Don't be idle for the earth will
continue to be a Gaia.
It is said.

This became humanities enlightenment
the relics of the clans that pushed God's
word.

Leaving Earth

Saint Ursula

The unlucky Saint Ursula was the lead of
the 11,000 virgins reputedly martyred
at Cologne, now in Germany.

By the Huns, in the 4th-century nomadic
invasion of southeastern Europe.

The Struggle Of Women

Once upon a time,
we were supreme.

Out came foreign.
Flipped on us the
power of our own
being.
The struggle of women,
now broke us.

Once upon a time:

We would choose our men.
We would choose when.
We would control the family.

Violence on land made us
secondary.

Never envy us, all men.
Our strengths are delicately
woven in with softness.
Our struggles are pain
beyond belief.

Humbled has become us!
Our spirits are chained as
our core sits on its course.
Torn are our souls, ripped inside
with the life we bring.

All we ask from God
is simply one thing.
If we return make our
lives more bearable so
we can eat.

The Tears Of A Woman

Earth Became My Zoo

Help I am in a massive
cage.
Earth has become a
holding cell,
called my zoo.

God I curse you every
living day.
Why place me here?
The animals I deal
with in this way.

Torment my spirit
behind these bars.
Gods eyes are my
only vision of
those who pass by.

No different than a caged
animal but this time
human.
Another place observes
us daily.

An understanding of the
type of dopamine I need,
to prevent me from
going crazy.

Depress is my spirit.
I don't vocalize.
Feel me, I internally scream,
in this cage I wish to die.
In the end I know as a human
we can go out and flutter.

Then I think, an attempt to heal
what about those in our
surroundings?
Really stuck in a cage of steel.
Our animals; one of past karma
now merely part of human dominated
lives?

Maybe to better ourselves
the least we can do
is increase consideration.

Recognize the show.
And make our own worlds,
more unpolluted with love and
compassion.

Sensory And Compassion

A Secret

Deep in the dark corners of
private offices everywhere,
academia gives leaders
the statistics of our truthful plight.

We are this short on water,
barrels of oil have dropped.
Tundra's baselines are royally being cut.
Please can you help maintain
us to prevent further ecological
disasters.

The light continues:

> *Furthermore, how do we tell women*
> *the grisly truth?*

> *When love hits the feminine,*
> *Many feel it's the baby*
> *that makes the man*
> *fully glued.*

> *1,2,3, and 5..*
> *The role of religion or the sadness*
> *behind this immense lack of control.*
> *How do we verbally communicate,*
> *this heavy reproductive toll?*

As women, we hold hands and
stand in front of you so humbly.
Words of wisdom, empowerment
and prayers for other starting so
innocently.

We have a secret, voices of reason say,
we have a strength that can be
modernized in the best of ways.

The rule of thumb is academia
needs to guide us. To illustrate
long term collective sustainability.

Progression means knowing
the womb and the notion to
stay away please.
Stop doing global fierceness men
and let women vocally be.

To the bearing females we guide always.
Regardless of who the love is.
Ladies, remember!
In general, two buns and your done
philosophy.

Never forgetting ancestry is really a
a 25-year responsibility.

This will design a better world
for both you and me.
It will also make the world of men,
not be covertly managing and actually
have faith in humanity.

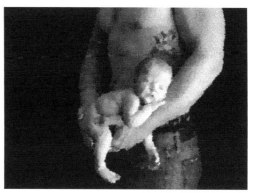

The Value Of Human Life

I Grip Your Head Tight

Love is beautiful but
today is my way.
I mark your back and
grip your head with my
strong arms.

Furiously I make love to you,
the testosterone in me that
was way over due.
The skies don't judge us
for even the animals
do the same.

We were all made equal
from the soils that germinated
this truss.
What others view in modern
times as a shame.

Our Love

Whose Monkey is the Better Monkey?

One monkey, two monkey, three.
Which one now became me?
Dr. Seuss you were the God,
I now take over from thee.

Once upon a time we had many
different monkeys.
Colors, their traits, even some fur
came blatantly through.

So much enlighten we lack,
education we now fight back.
The philosophical question that
reigns over us is, which monkey
is the better monkey of you?

Snowy were the ones from China.
Furry knuckles were the ones from Africa.
Round eye chimpanzee mixed in
also entered Europe and Anatolia.

Are all these monkeys confusing you;
because we can even throw in a tail
or two, in all of this migrational stew.

Compete we did for centuries.
Outburst of violence and fights,
different races we got confused and
encroached the many.
The confusion of genetics to what
made up an enemy's bite.

If we think about it,
Adam and Eve were not really
Biblical, if we see the academics behind
what is really right.

Cross reference don't you dare.
Little did humanity know we
were designed from monkey's traits,

in one massive animalistic delight.

I Love My Genetic Traits

The Greek Goddess

Real woman you were, with hips so
wide.
North Africa's whites were some
of your oldest lineage.
Anatolia made your ancestral people's
resting place, a blend of all three
continents.

Your curly long blonde hair,
olive skin became the exotica of a
phenotype designed by blue.

The thickness in your breast,
so succulent with no disguise.
Your beauty caused the Trojan
war and the series of omen injected
vengeance, of other women's cries.

Helena you were in spirit,
an infamy of true female,
and the desire of numerous
men.

An evolved Venus.
The earliest beginnings
of what became today
the Queen's of all the heavens.

A representation of all leads,
started on this planet
with wombs like you.
The essence of the first desiring
female Goddess, that others
simply pursued.

Helena, The Greek Goddess

Konyaliyim

A division of the ancient Greek people, even found in Hittite records. For over a thousand years, our family heritage was from Ionia.

We are the people of Konya, we proudly once said I am Iconyaliyim, Konyaliyim.

The Skatan

Skatan we hate,
not to be mean.
We have trouble,
feeding our might,
of 50,000 strong.

Skatan no more,
we leave your
violent manners.
The rules of God,
are now encoded in our soul.

Civilized we are,
democracy and philosophy
we bring to light.
Far from your ways,
of primitive delight.

Bitter turns to mockery
call it centuries of ill.
Skatan turns to skata,
and that is our will.

Dancing Around The Fire

A Mix of Three, We Became Thee

A petite island, 200 Km,
in the Mediterranean Sea.
Is our Crete.
Minoan is its history.
Its people are a mix of three,
from one end to the next.

When confused Anatolians would say:
"From one end of Crete, to the other end
of Turkey" (Ya Hanyaya, ya Konyaya).
They strongly still professed!
But let's not forget Africa, in all of this
bless.

Many things have come and gone.
Rich became their story.
The historic divisions of four became
their small regional territory.

Khania, Rethimnon, Iraklion and Lasithi.

Where Khania is now
pronounced Hania, but Konya is
still Konya,
Gone today are the variations and
mockeries.

Modified may be their language,
cultural heritage is their story.
Ancient Egypt and Mesopotamian
trading, was the center, once upon
a time of their glory.

But mixed of three are their people.
Crete from one point to the next.

Minoan Goddess

The Fight For Artic

Our land was so quite,
ships would even
have a hard time
passing through.

Our people, of Inuit and Eskimo
extraction; lived off whale blubber,
and raw fish.
Sunlight either too much
or too little.
Would determine the light
for kilometers away.

Then one day,
a few too many ships
started passing through.
Man did so much
damage abroad.
They began searching here,
hoping to resolve all
their woes.

They started disturbing
the underground.
Cracking the ocean floor.
What on earth were
they looking for?

Fix your own surroundings.
We represent tribes of
the Greenlandic people
and want to remain clean.
Not in between your battles and
environmental wars.

Davis Strait

New Grandada

I took my friend Ada
to Grenada,
The local said "*are*
you grand like our island of 1498?"
A corny joke came blaring through.

She said "African I am",
Proud is my heritage.
But never forget
so are you.

The local laugh,
sugar and spice,
and everything nice,
is our island.
Cod and bakes are
our happy food.

Smells cinnamon, clove and nutmeg,
every single day of the year.
All part of our ethnic food.

Vibrant in colors is our people.
Tropical now has
become our flavor.

Like everyone else who left
the mother land.
Just a different time, and one of
an unethical plan.
A different culture is what we
grew into.

My great grand papa was even
born here, this is all we knew.
I am a proud Grenadian hope I am
not sounding rude.

More simply put,
does Africa have any of these plus
some punch-a-rum, too?

Hillsborough

G17- Guam

Chukchi Nomads Of Guam

We are the Chukchi. Part of the Paleo-Asiatic nomads

Our Penis's roamed Siberia, Guam and the coast off British Columbia.

G18- Guatemala / Republica De Guatemala

I Love God

A transformed angel with wings and might.
Wrap me now, and hold me real tight.

Like an eruption, I begged for life
I can't breathe.
My love for him is that deep.
Many dark clouds later I discover.
All the benefits that I will now reap.

I love my God,
a hand he had loan.
Lifted my spirits,
those that were torn.

I dictate a section of Miguel Angel
Asturias to him,
like a sorry song:

> I woe to him, Lord,
> he who doesn't exhaust his supply,
> And, on returning, tells you:
> "Like an empty satchel
> is my broken heart."

When you look at dark and nothing
makes way. When a void fills your world.

Just love your God
inhale his power,
that is all I have to say.

A transformed Angel

Guinea Fowl

Good morning my friend,
how many eggs did you produce
for us?

We really need to eat!
For centuries you are
definitely God's blessing
to humans.

Stay close to home the
big cats, snakes and civets
may also want to eat.

Our reason is, he who steals
an egg will steal more.

Traditional African Religion

Our traditions are oral rather
than scriptural.
We chant and dance.

We believe in a supreme
creator.

The practice of blood sacrifices, omen
spirits, veneration of ancestors,
use of magic, and traditional medicine.

In our hearts most of us ignore
what foreigners injected into
us.

Our four ethnic groups Balante,
Fulani, Mandyako and Malinke
are all different, in format of practices.

But some still have ancient customs
we call real traditional African religion.

Our faith determines the spirits,
we try to restore.

Balante Female

Sleep Peacefully Mama

I am a Proud Guyanese!
Proud Afro-Guyanese,
to say the least.

Indentured slaves were
the other half of the people
that were brought.
My great grandmamma rest in peace,
was even Amerindian.

Our recorded country name
came from them they would say.
Land of water, but I believe it actual
originates from early slavery.

An anchorage stop that brought in our
first black slaves. Disembarking them
to an area of their origins in France,
port Guyenne, synonymous with their land
of water -Aquitaine. That the Dutch gradually
picked up.

A blood wrapped infant she was
when she was immediately
separated at birth.
Little is known of her earliest,
other than the few words of
what the land tells us today.

A remembrance she would do
to even her late second mother,
a negro female nicknamed dada.
The small handful of memories
of what would have been a
women closest to her as a mother figure.

The many tales told to her at night in the
crowded chattel sheds.
Goosebumps as she would recount
recollection of her own great Amerindian

history through the narrated, word to mouth
stories.

Wonderful feelings would whiz into her, sitting
amongst the wild flowers in her
vivid thoughts. The blow horn of shell
to call one region to the next.

Ana from the stories of her great forefathers
they would say, mother earth is the highest of
all the females on this land.
Their words of wisdom are what you should heed.

Wondering since my own childhood about
all the females on my mother's side I barely
knew.

How I wish, I would wail.
Just to touch the black silky hair.
May you find peace in your spirits
as I call out to all of you,

I kneel and pray.

-H-

H1- Haiti

Red Voodoo

Painted faces,
eyes rolled back.
Straw dresses.

Combined with chants,
and animal sacrifices,
we do all this to
transform reality.

Our sacrificial red
is our favourite colour.
The one that stirs iron
and fire.

We dance and ask the
spirits to bring us
back the ones that
are with our flyers.

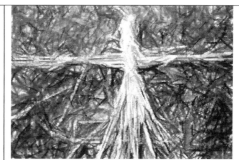
Voodoo Doll From Straw

H2- Haiti

Behind the mountain there may actually
be another mountain.

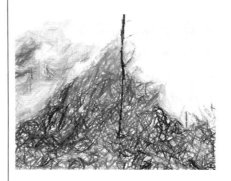
Pic Macaya

The Secret Lines

Cuneiform tablets, buried deep in soil.
Everything flatten on top of
the mountain's heavy toll.

An archaeologist said in 1934,
these are Indo European
words on Turkish soil!
He read slowly, the lines on the clay scrolls.

Nu Ninda-an ez-za wah a-tar-ma.

I felt a correction of work had to be made.
Studying, for fun, the earliest dialogues of
our forefather's today.

They were a panel of professors sitting
gracefully. May I add with humbleness
please.
Can I present the very sad, centuries of
hidden their chi still in the breeze?

Understand these ancient and very
old written scrolls.
There is more to the nail chip
by hand and baked clay, the
marks found on Anatolian soil.

These are slow transitions from one
language to the next.
The dying of languages and the
changeover of our phonetic co-share
words from our shamanic best.

Some came from the east; others came
from the west! Hundreds of thousands
of years' prior sounds were naturally
incorporated in the heart of what was
once the Hittite Empire. The marks above
similar to Ephesus should now read:

Nu Ninda-an ez-za wah a-tar-ma.

*The kings said upon entry,
follow the path of holy water.
Our point is the one that is
closest to God.*

Anatolia's known as one of the oldest crest,
these words made up an ancient world's
earliest cleanse.

Today these regions can be known as the the
temporary home of English's language first
dialogue structures.

Cuneiform Tablets

Beyond The River Hebrus

Akkad's we are.
The streams for pathways
we followed.

Damaged papuk,
our feet worn.
We try to wash each dead,
in one tributary
and drink from the other.

Following the animal trails,
to nourish our tired souls.
Looking for our only means of
survival the meandering Ak,
of streams and pathways.

Our only true judgment,
is our needs.
The hills for our spirts,
what the land provides
and the life we call holy, springs.

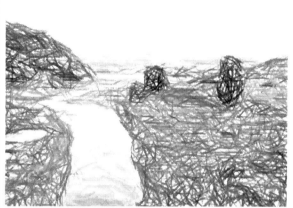

Rendition of Hebrus River

Captain Henry Morgan

Goodbye Elizabeth. Don't wait!
Loving you brought passion to
my soul but understand the only
loyalty I can profess is to my King
and my country.

You are a beautiful woman but my job is
horrendous. Our many fleets get emerged
underwater, we have even lost a few at
sea.

The waves are as high as mountains.
The gigantic surfs make the strongest
of our men who can even lift our six
feet anchors feebly ill.

Find another passion you only deserve
the best and wipe your tears.
Our battles with the Spaniards in
Panama was an encounter that nearly
cost me my life. There is a good chance
I may not return.

This time Las Barbaras awaits us, we
have to carry live cargo and our men
get very ill with their diseases on board.
It is so bad when we disembark the locals
have to give us lime to prevent hurling
and have even nicknamed us limey's
for looking that green.

I will give you some advice Elizabeth
it is the secret of all Seamen, never ever
put your heart and love a Captain again,
especially ones that carries the stripes
that represent the "*Kingdom of Lions*".

Weeks abroad

We are almost on shore, now men be very
careful! These local women are beautiful.
Their long strait black hair, almond
piercing eyes and strong legs will entice
you. Do not commit mutiny, you must
remain dedicated and loyal to your
country.

You may unchain the deceased left on
broad and clean the feces two days from
now. Until then our live cargo gets
released first. Have some compassion,
they are sitting in urination and blood for
weeks and are deathly sick.

Our job is to protect England's interest
first.

§

Captain "Sir" Henry Morgan 1674

*You, Sir Henry Morgan have been so
dedicated to your country, privateer they call
you. We beg to differ. Your act of courage
especially against the Spanish made our
country bow are heads in respect and honor.*

*I, King Charles, have now appointed you as a
hero to the British Empire and Monarchy.
May your title always represent the highest
civility we will give to the world.*

Counting Sheep

We own this land,
safe we thought ourselves
in the mountains.
These barbarians have ransacked
everything!

They took grain,
set the 3 village homes on fire.

The worst is they scared all our
sheep. 1,2,3,4 and 19 all jumped off
the cliff in Kekes.

No compassion these animals had,
Can you imagine our wound when
they only stole three.

Now we have no food to eat.
How we pounded on the icy soil
and cried.

All we do nowadays is suffer with
Famine and at night count sheep to
let the cold winter months pass us by.

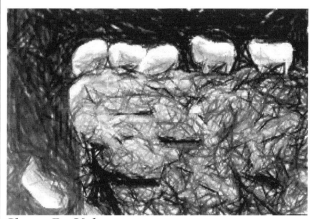

Sheep By Kekes

-i-

The Dolls Of Iceland

Everyone's vision of beauty
is different.
Each culture that comes and
goes has a makeover
that represents inner soul.

Some were designed rarer than
others, this you should
know.
Increasing the mathematics
of demand in attractiveness
of the bold.

The Dolls of Iceland

Made of glass and snow.
God added the bleu,
a rarity so deep it belongs
with a crown in a chateau.

In the end perfection is what
is bestowed.

The Dolls of Iceland

Were given to us by the skies.
To match the crystal hues of the
sparkled flakes on the icy land,
to where they were born.

Ram Is My Kar

Ram is my Kar,
whose head sits on the platter.
The nightly dances of headdress,
each manhood dances with.

The wind that wakes up,
the scent of those that
are in need.

Ritual after ritual,
blood drips.

Scorned are the heavens
in the sacrifice, they call
kur ban.

Yet hopeful are those,
that pounders over
the meat provided.

Ram is my Kar
that is feasted upon.

Decorated Kur ban

The Revolution

We see the light and
social ethics were born.
Eco-warriors is the Shiva
of fierce spirit in us.
We are sick of everything
suppression is no more.

The study of human social
behavior, came out.
This time using language
and what historically went wrong.

A path of green warfare
Social justice
Connecting DNA
Merged are these concepts together
Angry to high hell,
we all are.

Revolution of the womb,
survival it has now become!

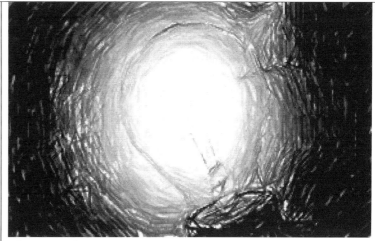

The Revolution

I4- India

Sanskrit

Kind and gentle words makes everyone happy,
take this papyrus and try to
write the earliest phonetics
to give to humanity.

Bha, Li, Mu, Ni, Ri, and Za

Papyrus Papers

I5- India

Ignore Monogamy

We are indigenous wild and free!
We love the forces of life.
Whites first invaded us
3,500 years ago.

We told them and our scholars
the same,
ignore monogamy we want to
make love to everybody.

Temple of Love India

Sun Temple Konârak

Shaman we are,
we lift our palms to the sun
and we ask of you.
Find us relief from the destructive
forces around this land.

We carry this tiny body.
A common occurrence
of illness which took his life,
from the land.

Unlike others,
he was born to earth badly
deformed.
We knew he would not last
and was an evil from those
who screech at night in the forests.

His soul will not be fed to the flying
ones in the skies.
We will simply chant and dance.
That the demons, like the bewitched
women who made him don't come
by.

Wc will rip both mother and son
apart and give this omen to the
woods.
Reptiles will consume both of them
and we pray others like them will
never
reincarnate.

Konârak you represent ancestry and
the one in our skies.

Depiction of Konârak

The Living

Ever see the magic inside
a rain forest shimmer?
Colour laden are its vapour
filled mist.
So delicate is its land.

A rainbow god would have
had to have merged land
and sky.
Done with love and
his hard labour.

Burnt orange are its orangutans,
baby blue are its fish.
But there is something
you should know.
Lethally deadly, that should not
be missed.

Clay are its dead soils,
delicate cover it needs.
Pangea once attached the land
before the split of all the
turbulent seas.

Lift the trees and its suckers,
desert will be its
new name.
Know the value of compost,
Sahara was once lush and the same.

A membrane so dark and
delicate, earth needs to
survive.
Protect it with vengeance to
mystify the skies.

Mother Earth Holding Water

Assassin

We wait for the monstrous
enemy on the hill top.
Fall bait to us please,
we have no mercy.

Sold was our secrets
to the kingdom.
Our messengers did they
kill.
Blood wars did ours become.

Come in, come in.
Show a blank face.
Feed them hashish,
then kill them slow.

Europe will one day
make this famous,
and transform hashshashin,
to assassin.

A word to remember this
fierce enemy's blow.

Hideout Zagros Mountains

The Three Prayers And One Sacrifice
of Elam

The elder came in the tent.
You have to give him to us!
No, the women wail.
It has been 20 moons,
she is not going to recover.

She has lost a lot of blood.
The elder man snatches
the infant. The five brothers
follow him to base of the
Elam plains.

They put the male infant on an
Altar and commence
sacrificial rituals of Anshan.
The dances of manhood begins.
Ones to make clan men
strong.
The others to remove omen.

Dear sky Gods, we are giving
you back to him,
for the lost of Yacoub's
concubine.

Just when the dances hit
night, a child comes running over.
The mother has awoken,
please stop.

She is wailing and will
poison herself if the infant is
not brought back.

The men think the women
are attempting to outsmart them.
Into the animal hide tent they all burst into.

Please elder, I kiss your hands, a voice faintly
whispers by the candle glimmer.
The mountains sent my spirits back

May I hold my firstborn, please.

The men then brought the full
fed newborn back to Elam plain, the next
day.
On the altar they gently placed
him.

They kept his tiny body wrapped;
in the same white linen, as a reminder
of how unlucky he may have been.
Called the white linen of death.

Ezra, is now your name.
A reminder of the mountain's heaviest
toll on us.
A small mark we will do
on your forehead with a knife.

You will never have to do the ritual
of manhood at the passing of 14 different
seasons.

They lift the child high above their heads,
we are grateful Elam for not bringing us
darkness and for granting us our blessings.
We thank you for not taking one more of
our dead.

Feeding The Sun God

Married to my first born daughter,
we know no better.
Then to go to the hilltop
where she will lead.

A place magnificent to see,
Mayan my beautiful queen
how I love you.

May your blood dripping
be the chastity, to feed the Sun
God.
May your body coil around me
to keep us warm.

Your hair of youth,
will wrap both of us.
Married to my first born daughter,
we know no better.

How I will enjoy thee.

Ottoman Head Quarters

Sultan, we will set up three critical
points.
Vienna we went all the way up to
and was given the hardest front.

Yet we still couldn't access their gates.
Mosul, Konya, and Basra are now our
new headquarters.

North Africa was always our
territories.
Istanbul we acquired in 1453.
We still want Europe what
should we do now?

Gather all the foreign women caught,
throw them in my Harem.
Kaya Kadin will calm all of them
down.

If they do not bend to us,
we will weaken them by
showing their ancestry
what could have been.

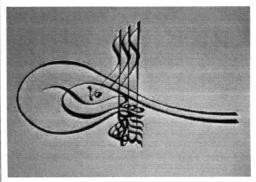

The Sultan's Signature

Tribal We Are

Barbarians they say we are, they do
not understand shaman warfare and
what is hunger?

We come into Al Amarah
and it is the first crossroad of another
tribal clan.

What is the first thing we look for,
even before to eat.
Are the women we wish to
plunder.

Our manhood will protect them
to carry our lineage.
Self preservation is the marry!

Henna Decorated Tribal Women

Uri

I see the full moon but await
till everyone is asleep.
I sneak out;
my tender breast makes me
the youngest of the entire
family tree.

In the dark I hear my name
softly, Uri are you there?

My lover a man more than
two times my age.
Love at first sight,
he grabbed me violently during
water collection. I fell for him.

You know I will die a million
deaths for you, I touch his
hardened cheeks.

The mountains have to forgive us for
the love we make.
Next season they want to marry me.
He stares blankly at me while he
pulls out of me.

We are a different tribe, Uri
and they refused the bride price
we offered to pay.
Don't sacrifice yourself, my love
to the Gods he says.

Marry him.
Cut the womb gently inside
with chopping chisels. Glue it with a mix of
lemon, bark sap and sugar.

They will never know,
that your price was lower.
Then poison him slowly.

As a short lived widow,
they may find you omen

and wish to forgo you.
Beg for life.
Cry you never had love for him.
You wish to live.
Then we will continue our
love.

Uri we have no where we can go.
The mountains, the moonlight in
darkness is our only sacred home.

Al Qurnah Region

Castle On Inishmore

Once upon a time the Celtics
settled in Anatolia.
A connector point was this
warmer land. They could not take a
dwelling or two.

If we do not leave,
violence will be the death of us.
It will continually ensue.

A few thousand years later,
they blended many times violently with the
migratory indigenous of the region.
Where they then permanently settled up
north.

The low lands were very cold,
but fish was abundant.
"We can change some of these
rock type Henges," they said to be an
extremely strong and safe fort.
Visiting Ireland, you should see some of the:

    Old Turf home blended into
    Ireland's landscapes,
    cultures exhibits
    and its monuments so great.

But if you want a spiritual link, I mean one
that connects humanities' soul.
 The words their forefather's carried reflects
the footsteps of our earliest, earthy first
faiths.

Take a side trip to Aran island.
There perched on an edge,
Innishmore you will find the 200ft cliff.
Still very indigenous called hungry bird, Dun
Acngus. Part of what is a remembrance to that
of our historical dead.

Walk slow and just imagine 8,000 years ago,
the struggle of humanities past.

That cliff they fed their family
a most strikingly imaginable path.
Stay on its tip, if you may and
look to the sky and feel the breeze.
The view from its rampart.

Now imagine, how they let go of
their spirits,

Simply feel their ancient shamanic tease.

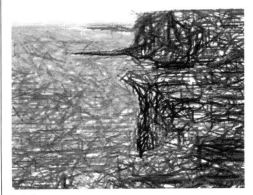

Inishmore

Adam or .....

In a region of antiquity far away,
many traversed and
was one of the oldest
in countless ways.

Hava, Awa meant skies
but so did Eve,
found everywhere lets study
this female she....

Adam and Eve you were
born biblically.
Did you ever wonder if
there was actually more to thee?

Israelites are the chosen's
it is said in the Bible.
The only ones first link to Ivri
(pronounced Eve-rih)
Now I sit and wonder?

Sounds like the first spirit of womb
when we decode this in our head.
Rih is the energy in her soul
that was wrongly fed.

Even back then the source of life,
were the female Venus's in lead.
The mother of all of earth,
our historical missing key.

If we look at this anthropologically
the story merged together
transformed itself to a biblical she.

A distancing from any animal,
as a female brought the first he.

The clue is in Hebrew Ivrim another
connecter to her now sacred bed.
A possession of life, one that meant
Holy, to the ones that profusely bled.
Ivri today belongs to the start
of her spirit and her soul as Eve.

Humans had to separate when
a conscious was actually born,
so for centuries when no written existed
this is the story that was told.

One day it became encoded
in all the prophecies from above.
Christ's acknowledge the chosen people
well and gradually transpose, our Eve and
humans to only a single deity.

The rule of God in revealing human
 then became the story of what
is the sacred apple that cast the
first spell.

Adam and ....

Ahu'di

Ahu'di we look at the sky,
our feathers in different array.
Painted faces we howl to the moon.
Don't use your might or your claws,
omit us from any type of pain.

Ahu'di we rip skin,
a painful ritual to become men.
Our finger nails still carry
the flesh of manhood.
To show you our strengths.

Ahu'di we ask,
"why do you devour our dead"?
Eat our food we kill for you
instead.

Masada the hilltop of sacred feast.
We ask you to bring them back.
Ahu'di became your mark,
the power of your fame.

Sketched Diagram of a Jewish Bird Sculpture.- ahudi (yahudi) is Anatolian people's reference to early bird believing Jews. It still means Jews today. Anything prior to 5,000BC.

The Elder Of Safad

Elder why do you sit by this
Synagogue for hours.
He would say,
I find great peace secluded
in here.

This is the oldest synagogue in the
region.
The Sephardic Ari
and represent healing for me.
It connects me back to God,
our cemetery of ancestry is
a remembrance
just two minutes away.
A closeness I really need.

Elder you still have a family spend time
with them.
My protection of family is not needed.
My children are all grown and
my life is God now, with my other half
gone.
The reading of the Torah makes
me strong.

This is where I wish to die.
An odd pleasure I feel as the
breeze hits my soul.
Let my homage and respect to
that of the skies
be what is the best for me,
the keeping of spirits, as a whole.

Our Elder By Safad

The White Lion Of Golan Heights

Once sacred was your home,
able to tackle down a large
elephant alone.

The other beasts did not torment you
on that soil that also use
to freely roamed.

How green was the land you
once had
called your own.

The Golan mountains use to say:

O sanctuary, a place you have made home.
We will do a homage to a King,
in these Royal lands.

You make the valley's weep with the
fierceness you bestow.
Arise and go forth let people feel
your spirit.

White lion stood sacred and alone.
Mighty was your kingdom,
the essence of what was now
transformed.

The White Lion Of Golan Heights

Yehudi

Conquest was our might,
holy is our land.
Yehudi are the ones
we collected globally.

Our land was protected.
We roam, free to be.
Now by divine's touch,
chosen became our spirits.

From pointed grunts to
looking at the moon.
To Ivri the birth of Hebrew.
Hanna was our first,
Star of David was our eldest.
Our forefathers followed the thin
animal trails.

God's will for Canaan,
Divine's resolve and
perfect aim.
Our ten hands still touch the
skies.

Blessed were we,
merged together.
Holiest sites we pray.

To others we say: "*We are the chosen
people belonging to the promise land,*

Eretz Tzion v' Yerushaliyim"

Yehudi

The Seven Day War

Annex was this war,
called the six-day war.
To grow our holiest land.

God blessed,
its people with a call.
That there were many
other regions to commemorate.
To say they were the forgotten
ones.

Made in Ahri'da,
her birth year was also 1967.
One day more, than the six-day
war and seven should then
become their luckiest.

A reminder call and whisper that
said..

"Do not forget, the
ones who's spirits hid in the mountains.
The many regions whose forefathers,
fully developed language.
They also roamed.

The synagogues in these district,
their other first settlements.
Cultural artefacts left behind
equally important as the holy lands".

A prayer's call is needed.
For the spirits of the forgotten.
They innocently said to the mighty
rulers at that time.

We are the proud people,
we are Yerushaliyiz.

A private message to Israel from the author
regarding their Ottoman history and the
conflict of what is defined as a cultural
heritage.

Ottoman Jews

Marco Polo

Its 1271 and we are in Indian territory.
Venetia all the way to the east.
I have education and a good knowledge
of their Koman dialects.

In the freshness of the night,
they point and say it quick.
Hindi is some sacred site,
all in the north.

It doesn't matter, we still cut across.
All their territories,
Yunnan, Kafiristan and Cathay
to name a few.

Travel we do from one
point to the next.
Koman is their dialects,
and I am the first European to
reach all the way through.

Marco Polo Travelling, In a Tatar Outfit

Roma's Mark

Polygamy,
Bestiality,
Art,
Cathedrals,
Heels and whips!

Roma's ancient and
trendy culture.
Really hip.

Pasta,
Grape vineyards,
Leaning towers,
Aqueducts
and
Historical fleets of ships.

These are the social
marks of a culture.
Today in full fashionable tips.

Designed by centuries
of artistic genius
and fashionable
illumination.

Roma's ancient and
trendy culture.
Really hip.

Early Human and Goat, Sexual Indecency.

J1- Jamaica

The same bird that will carry news,
will be the same bird that will fly back.

Jamaican Tody (Todus Todus)

J2- Jamaica

Bob Marley

Identity is what is designed when people
had no media and became individuality
of
one of a kind.

A tiny island in the Caribbean Sea.
For four hundred years became the way,
of its highest in spiritual blue peaks.

A genre of music that was called the
consciousness to the extreme.
From a descent of slave.
Lyrics of a true soldier that gave way to
our global heritage gift.

Heard even in the smallest of pubs in
Tokyo.
May he rest in peace.
A person who became an example
of expression of individuality
beyond belief.

Bob Marley

J3- Japan / Nippon

Osaka

Don't you know shaman, Osaka
is the region for purification of
spirits;
the place we call our meandering
holiest of waters?

Our ancient rituals of death.

Osaka Wan

J4- Japan

Shintoism

My power is the most
potent of all weapons.
It is the analytical capacity
to know divine spirits.

These are from the teachings of
our earliest nature worships.
Even before the many prayers
of celestial were created.

Japanese Shinto Structures, Starting 6th
Century

We never forget the divine,
goodness given to us by
God.
Where misfortune is averted
and sickness is healed.

We only blame ourselves
for the lack of teachings.
We are the ethical content
who will now fulfill our
obligations to our ancestors.
In believing!

Dry River Valley

Sandstone and granite are its
mountainous surroundings
of heights of over 1,700m.

Its narrow gorges, fissures of carved
natural arches and 25,000 rock carvings.

Once upon a time there was a flowing
interaction with our natural environment.

Wadi Rum was the place of cover,
that even the seven pillars of
wisdom were written about.

Its shamanic name was once known
as the cool flowing river valley.

Part of Rift Valley

-K-

Dark Wings, Black Nights

Lethal is your span.
You have become our symbol of
warfare.
Chants do we do to you,
in the tundra of the night.

Beet soaked flags with charcoal,
adorn were our first drawn in wings.
Power we ask from you.
Our blow banners change,
with each of the directions
when we followed you.

Only wings do we carve
in our armours and coats.
An emblem of hidden past;
a struggle of our silent foes.

Dark wings, black nights,
over thousands of years.
Became our heritage symbol.
Many of our forefather's
remembrance of battles
and tears.

Kazak Emblem

Hours Spent Studying Fingers And Sky

Man saw the skies,
and elaborated our devil has wings.
The thousands of years of transformation
to angel.
Where did this come from?
Half bird, half human.

He lingers over us like a dark shade,
they once had said.
The noises he makes.

Kik became his first name,
Uyu became the permanent
sleep he acclaimed.

Don't wake,
how they begged.

Kik uyu *sleep please*
Kik uyu *sleep please*
They quietly said.

We mimic you only to be fierce in battle.
The violence in other territories rage.
So many of us die.
How you devour our many dead?

Fear us, to others they howled,
like we fear the darkness that comes
from in the sky.

Kik uyu *sleep please*
Kik uyu *sleep please*
`
Only bring omen to the ones we desire.

Kikuyu Tribe, Africa

K3- Kiribati / Gilbert Islands

Magical Phoenix

When the sun goes down in
the Pacific Ocean.
The coral atolls shine,
and the waters underneath
all come to life.

Luminous the moon hits
the surface,
pristine are the life beneath
that never sleeps.

In the dark is when our Phoenix
comes out to eat.

The Moon in Tarawa

K4- Kosovo / Kocobo

The Ova Of Birds

We stand around a fire
in the region known as
black birds, and pray hard.
Mighty one, hear our souls.
We have seen so much
violence.

The "Ova of Birds" represents our spirit
that makes us stand tall.
It promotes skies.
Maybe one day in the future we
will reincarnate to a place called
the Raven's heaven.

The Might of the
Black Bird Emblem

Tragedy Of Life

The tragedy of life is not
death but what we don't
let go to the spirits.

Our tears, our wounds
created here on earth.

Higher than us.
The act of healing becomes us.
Take the dead to its proper
release at Bûbiyãn.

By these waters,
feed first the ones in the sky.
After the remaining bones are set
a flame,
crush the burnt bones and release
their past to the sea.

Then celebrate their
intermission of life.

Indigenous Burning And Crushing Of Bones

The Poet

Did Kyrgyzstan, think they had the only
poet in mind? Epic Manas, from the people
of Paleo-Siberian stock.

Were once influenced from runic- Turkic
writings, handed down from the bards, may
be the longest written script of 500,000
lines long.

But others have come and gone.
Which highlights, another version beyond.
A different theme of antiquity.
These are the many verses transversely
making up our shamanic history.

Vedic was inclined to be
their interesting blended traditions,
Zoroastrianism was the Pictionary of
their invisible scrolls.
Verbal also became, the stories of other
regions that were once told.

The oral literature of the first clans
that settled near Sulaiman mountains
highlighted the many stories so bold of all of
central Asia.

They said Turkic nation to Turkic nation,
were one example of the many varieties of
tribes that rolled.
Unique became these clans of human
now settled in these regionals zone.

Across the barren silk road,
which illustrates the richness
of each of these countries
hard existence and toll.

Customs so different and intricately deep.
Most people in the West
don't even know that Caucasus
features and even blue eyes slanted
makes up many of central Asia's
exotic mix.

Developed into cultural beauty of
art and poetry, gold covered antiques
of regional glare.

The base words from our history, all clan
dialect diverse, makes up only one component of
this region, to illustrate in this poem Kyrgyz's
beautiful
indigenous flair.

Altin Ara Shan

The One Million Elephants

Our people came centuries ago
from China in the 8th century.
Displacing the many tribes now
disdained as Kha.

Once in the mercy of dark lands
the Khmer Kingdom ruled the
entire region including neighboring
Thailand and Vietnam.

The 16th century onwards our lands
became attractive to Europeans.
We are humble people who still believe
in saffron outfits and the importance
of the Million Elephants at bay.

The Lucky Elephant

Walk Along With Me

Walk humbly with God
the Baltic spiritual way and
kneel, not just in darkness.

You were born the fruits
of labor.
The free men and women
against social injustice.
Don't ever let any blessings
be a dismissal.

A national awakening.
The skies will be your savior,
highest merit are those
born humble with flavor.

Walk along with me.
Your path will be gold and
righteous.

But always remember
pagan and the heavens
were our original ways.

The Gothic scripts of the 16th Century

Roman Style

Baalbek a Phoenician metropolis.
Roma came in 64BC.
And converted the triads of Heliopolis.
Jupiter, Venus and Mercury
from its name of origins
Baal, Anta and Alyn.

What an early monument was erected.
Representing the region known as Sun
worship derived from Greek mythology.
The many pilgrims it attracted to the
metropolis.
An entire city surrounded by
fifty granite-style columns.

Barbaric shamans they had said
"Learn from our ways".
We will never give up our altars
and religious temples, they yelled back.
But aggressive was Roma's impact.
Battle occurred daily in the region.

Converted may have been their historic
point.
Abandoned became their post.
Many new tribes changed over.
The city became permanent,
but the mark of heritage represented the
fierce warriors that are now ghosts.

What Is Death?

The Zulu tribes have attacked.
We expelled them out but darkness
falls over my soul as I stand over
the many graves.

In the middle of winter huddled
together, we take turns looking
blankly in the 4ft deep sloppy
excavated out trench.
Unlike recent times, Thabana
was the preference for their
forefather's burial place.

But gone are my belief in the skies!
An entire family.
How meaningless I think,
as tears pour down my face.

Freezing cold the weather is,
pretty are now the tribally
decorated bodies.

What is death? Weeks I have spent
morning.

When maybe I should celebrate?
And look at it like feeding back
the earth with the souls that are now
departed.

The Hand Of Death

Graveyard

I think therefore I am
There must be two of me.
A conscious and a being.

I told those immortal
not to worry!
One was for the sky; one
was for the sea.

In the end I will have left
everything.

Graveyard

Tour Guide To Tourist

We have so much heritage and
things of interest in Libya.
We also have in Tassili N'Ajjer an
evolution of changes that have
occurred in fauna and flora
over time.

*"We are so excited the tourist responds.
Do we get to see written of our earliest?"*

Oh no you get to see something even
better he responds. You will see an
order of succession of our first people of
earth and their recorded version of
changes over time on rock paintings.
The rocks of their soul and pain.

When Libya had elephants and
rhinoceros, magic religion scenes
and moist landscapes,
horses and very large plant life.

The oldest images recorded goes
back 14,000 years.

Our earliest forefather's struggles
and a reminder of their existence,
Ottoman politics and their unrested
shamanic strife.

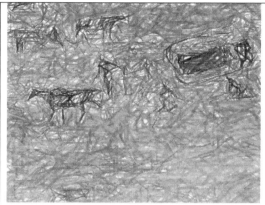
Unesco Tassili n'Ajjer Rock Paintings

Homage to Yacoub Aġa

Yacoub acquired a small
plot of land on Sechem and
erected a dolmen.

The brightest star is
the one I wish to follow,
his soul made him desire.

The whispers of my
forefathers before me.
Gave a chill down his
spine.

Surt to Odessa, they roamed.
Though one of the original
12 tribes all were unrelated,
except for one thing.
Unified they became with the
God Yahweh.

Perfection is the one
we desire in us.
Trading for a piece of
bread.
Transhumance for
greener pastures.

Tents we set up
to protect our concubines,
Ones we call our own.

Take a lead Yacoub Aġa.
Tonight you watch
over the many who sleep.

The Holy Bread

Liechtenstein	National Holdiay
Our country is small but proud we originate from the Alemani tribe.	We will get more revenue from parties, then we will do having a war. That is why an army is not required in our country this small. On our our national holiday, the serene Prince and Princess invite the entire country to the Vaduz Castle. Smiles and a beer is the flavour, if you have a business plan even better but tears on that day are not authorized at all. 

Follow The Path Of Light

It is 3:00 AM and I am in a vast land of
green known as the Curonian spit.
Trees are hovering over me.
Complete darkness in the forest
I stay still.

The moon is hidden, the single star
to the right is what the compass
arrow is showing me.
The trees whisper to me,
"*Dont be afraid*".

Look at this compass,
and follow this path of light.
The single star glowing,
leads me to the edge of the water.

The wind blows, and an
invisible hands freeze's me
all around.
The hazy mist sparkles,
tears pour down.
I realize then that I felt those
who use to roam here once
before me.

Follow The Path Of Light

Pressured from the Teutonic Knights,
we were the last pagan country in Europe.
Accepting Roman Catholicism in the late
14th century.
Some are ashamed, some are so proud,
better late than never the church once
yelled.

House of Burgundy

In medieval times, Henry VII
ceded to the "House of Burgundy".
The area once inhabited by all the
Belgic tribes.

Native clans which were part of
the highlands making up the
singing lands of even earlier,
there forefathers the indigenous
of Gutland (utlan).

Many wars ensued.
The Romans, Spanish,
even Germans
came marching right through.

Today its center quartier
sits as one of the oldest
fortifications.
A strategically military prize

This is a tiny land with a
written note of heritage.
The building of its people,
many centuries, of history,
science, folklore, art and literature.

The first advancement born from
what the Roman's nicknamed as the
Treveri tribes.

The Treveri Tribes

-M-

In Search Of Sanctuary

The kingdom of a very
ancient country.
Part of the Balkan peninsula.
Anatolia and Thrace are its
historic cultures so close.

The locals even have a mix.
A reminiscence of Ottoman influences
in the region.
Albanian, Serbs and Turks join in as their
minorities.

All recite this happy song:

In every heart there is a room,
a sanctuary safe and strong to
heal the many wounds.

Until a new day arises, may God
protect the borders of what we
call our own kingdom.

The place heaven made,
what our forefathers
knew.

The Sun And Spirits

Movement Of First Words

Ada is island in many countries
a word even found in Africa.

Cas is flexing of muscle of the ones
flying and found in South America

Gar means the mountains in
certain parts of Russia.

Kara globally means spirits of darkness

Merge together you get the etymology of
the earliest phonetics out of Madagascar.

Satanically translated,

The strength of the ones flying will be
found on the hilltops of this isle.

Is this a fluke or is this a coincident?
Only DNA merged with migration of
phonetics way in the future will tell us?

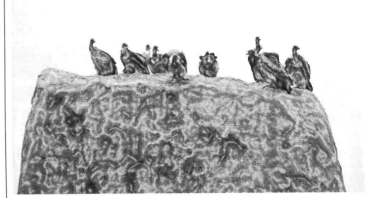

The Hills Of Madagascar

Bettering Thy Self

My greed swallows
me; I need the whole lot I say.
Ignore everything around me.
Diseased with survival,
is the only thing on my mind,
the ravens have betrayed

My family is in disarray.
My children refused to stay.
An infection has taken the best
of me.

A quiet hill on top of the
world. I ask the spirits please
help me, I can't handle this twirl.
The wind touches my face.
Grass tingles my feet,
a soul gently speaks:

   We come to this earth with
   a purpose, a call.
   Why do you feel you have to have it all?
   This is a tiny reminder, write it out if
   need.
   When you depart believe me,
   you will have nothing at all.

My tears I dry rapid
and bury my head in tender.
Oh spirits I say I was
not thinking about
the afterlife thunder.
   You are right
   we are not here long,
   I will heed your words of wisdom and
   wipe my tears, this death omen
   does not mean we are forever gone.

The Focus On Quality

The Language Of Birds

When we think of early humans and
the role of language historically.

Meaning the unknown or hidden
dialogues of
anything prior to 10,000 BC.

Academia wrote it off as just babbling.

Today the world was told we are all a
reminiscent of shaman! A constant that
once existed.

Don't believe the message from the souls
that are unrested?

We will now say don't be radical of your
past.
Even a Malaysian Blue-Rumped Parrot
with its minuscule bird brain can speak
human dialect.

Bue Rump Parrot

M5- Maldives

Stars Of The Indian Ocean

The hundreds of islands in the
Indian ocean tells us one important
thing about history.

*The journey of life and existence, its
beauty and vulnerability, and at night
the sparkle of its illuminated Sea Stars
had to have started off only by the magic
of the heavens and skies.*

Glowing Sea Stars

Emperor of Songhai

Mohammed was the founder of the Askia dynasty in 1495.

On his way to Mecca he was so impressed by the Egyptian pyramids he decided to construct a tomb for himself.

Upon my death, I want the people of these
Regions to remember me as the King of the Saharan Gold trade.

A genuine royal representing Africa and its people.

Emperor Songhai

The Purpose Of All The Prophets

The island 6000 years back, contained
seven megalithic monuments. The
representation of the development of
first culture.
The famous sites at the time were so holy
that these Malta stones, can even be
found in Anatolia.
Blessed to these structures they were
brought as blocks and carved delicately
with care.

Reforming beliefs of those of animals?
We are confused. The Carthaginians had
once asked:

"What purpose do you hold here"?

Each time period brings in another,
the locals responded. You came so that
we can be your salvation.

Think about it, what the world was like?
Let go of your emblems and violent ways
and believe in us.
The rocks represent our devotions.

We are a dominant empire of the region.
What purpose do the many prophets from the
region contain?

The Carthaginians continued.

They teach us, that there were numerous
people of divine and they are still here
but only in their spirits, the souls of what
was once revered is still felt today.

We always profess in our hearts, may
those who rule us for wisdom, always be
guarded.

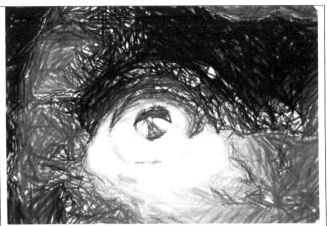
The Many Prophet

White Star

The 24 points in the median of
stars represent all our islands.
The sparkles from the skies
shines on each one individually.

Our people once had said
Ratak or Ralik?
Indigenous we are, we still do our
daily spirit communications.

In the morning at Sunrise Ratak,
in the evenings at sunset Ralik.

But it is our single White Star that
shines on all the isles that holds
our forefather's destiny.

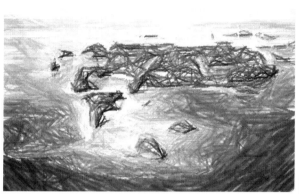

The 24 Isles Representing All The
Municipalities

Cross The Gibraltar

Cross the short strait of Gibraltar
and then use the caravans to reach.
There you will find the fertile
valley, a safeguard and resting spot
to hide the goods, we just brought
over.

Its ancient routes you can use,
to find the oasis trading post so
do not worry.
You wont miss it, the basin is
always clear.

By Ouadane's decorative entrance
you will find a papyrus note.

Follow clearly the directions and
give them the goods.
Take the message the messenger
from the other side has sent.

The map will lead you to the
treasures of gold.

Ancient Ksour of Ouadane

The Extinct Dodo Bird

Steal one egg from a Dodo
and you can feed five.

Steal three eggs from a Dodo
throw in some herbs and rock
smashed banana you can then
feed twenty.

The white man came now we can't
feed any.

This is a true story of how locals
lost so many.

The Extinct Dodo

M11- Mauritius

In Aapravasi Ghat the British did the
greatest experiment of all time, the site
was the place to use what they called
"free labour" instead of slaves.

We are now called free indentured
workers!

Babi-illim Our Watchtower (Babylon)

Your structure closest to the sky,
hovering in the horizon.
The ideals of our earliest,
be our watchtower.

Your shamanic name means
our door to enlightenment.
This light may it house our fears.
We feed the skies ban,
we sacrifice for knowledge.

The land of Shinar,
and still darkness falls over our
watchtower.
May the animal fat candle in your top
tower
be the call to follow Babi-illim.

Speak of the lessons of earth,
and bless us with the road to the skies,
the light and the tower.

Babylon's Historic Name – Earliest
Meaning Door To Enlightenment.

Transformed Fig Leaf

Fruits of our tree,
relish its sweetness we eat.
The symbolism of life,
the gift of fertility made you real.

Dear child,
how you were born with care.
Naughty are you today.
Sweet like sugar,
rambunctious like a baby lion cub.

The stems are the tussle
that binds your mother's hair.
The leaves are customs
of love that we do not tear.

Dear child,
product of a real warriors' fruitfulness.
The symbolic leaves of figs,
the average doesn't know!
Made Europe turned the symbol of
leaf to a heart for your loving beaux.

You are my ancestry today.

Transformed Fig Leaf

The Collapse Of Mayan

Region is Yucatan, 300AD.
The weight of the Gods are
so heavy.
We grind forest hallucinogenic
drugs to ease our pain.
The average age of our
elders are no more than 20.

We pray, help us!
We have exceeded the carrying
capacity of existence.
Droughts are heavy,
and disease has started to
flourished.

Delicate is our soul.
Afterlife we do believe in.
Lets us all agree and do a
blood sacrifice to the Gods.
Find a spare spot each.
And say hello to those before us.

So when we reincarnate,
our lives will not be
in such pain.

Gone did we become
yesterday.
The pyramids are the
death monuments
that will still await our new stay.

The Pantheon Of Nature Gods- Uxmal

M15- Mexico

Chihuahua how we would dance, the Maize dance!	

M16- Micronesia

Agana When the sleeping women awakes these mountains will move. The lead of all vagina's.	

The Meat Of A Walnut

Take a walnut it is moist, wet
and raw inside.
Plant it and out comes the
tree.
This tree knows it roots;
and that it was born
from a seed.

It harbours the meat of
those who eat it.
Why is its meat so
important?

Other than all the benefits
of nutrition it provides.
It represents a brain.
When de-shell and not
in disguise.

This brain represents
humanity you see.
You came as humans,
from a single seed.

This is now the analogy
of defining what is human
utilizing a root and a tree.

The walnut came out of its shell
And did not like its shell.

Was the amusing irony of race dissection
historically.

The Human Analogy

Honour Thyself

If we were hated by
an army of million,
we wouldn't care.

We know our faith
our destiny.

Honour ourselves.
In all of delight.
By the Grace of
God's will.

With reputation
we built our royalty.

The land of activity
everyday of the
year by the sea.

With no airport there.

The Honour Of Royal

Centre Of The Hunic Empire

Temujin has united all the
Mongol tribes.
One noble will be chosen to marry
Musa's daughter, his friend.

Hand to hand was she given after
The defeat of the Tatars, followed
by the great entry into the
Persian Gulf.

Master warriors were all of them
in fight, arches vigilantly developed.
Large stallions groomed with care.
The merging of the two leaders
became their sacred promise.

To control the dynasties of all
the surrounding kingdoms,
were their mottos.
They travelled by horse many
vast lands.

*Death and vengeance struck one
down.*

Musa's daughter then produces 7 more.
The spirit of his friend was now
Restored.

*Dedicated to My warrior son, Temujin. In
English Teymor*

Genghis Khan (Temujin)

Black Mountains

The Black mountains, the old region
known as Karst.
Talk to us what have you seen?

Our earliest buried food under
ground, cracked were their hands
with no shovels.
Fingernails of dirt and splinters.
By the fresh water outlets
they would sleep.

They would ask us, oh spirts of
darkness
to be kind to their humble souls!
Oh how we would be ruthless and
have
fun with all of them.

Back then our mountains had
a different name.
The Venetians came and switch
the game.

The cycle of life is funny you see,
the Ottomans marched in 1389, and
mixed up all their cup of tea.

World War One and Two,
we have seen it all.

We are just the Goblins of Dark
who just keeps carrying away,
the spirits of death.

The Blackened Mountains, All Ten
Fingers For Prayer To Them.

Gua, Hua or Dua

Dear friend you travel
so many miles.
Your faith is so different
from mine.

But yet you show interest
in Dua,
what possess thee?

"God is the same", she replies
We cross all lines to make
a difference.

You need prayer in your life.
It is same message but different
formats, that is really ok.
I will change my Hua to Dua
just for this visit I do here.

Dear tourist all the way from
Central America
Your Amerindian faith is so different from
mine.
But yet you show interest in
the mosques we have here.
What possess thee?

"The structures are all different", he replies
we historically have cross many boundaries
of war over religion,
but today I would like to respect
your house of God.
I kneel my head, like you. We can merge our
prayers together".

For you just this week, I will change my
ancient spirituality of Gua to Dua.
Just for the visit I do here.

Dear Student all the way from Botswana,
our faith's are so similar.
But yours is a different sect and has
culturally different customs than mine.

Come into this little mosque this time.
My African friend politely declines.
Let me try to convince you otherwise.

For many years,
I have brought in many people to this
family run bed and breakfast by the water.
I have never been on a plane, have formal
education or have really left town.
This area is all I know.

But I want to teach you, how I have been
educated from the many who come and go.

I have learnt that strangers can hold remarkable
kindness.
I have seen tolerance of differences
beyond the told.
I have learnt from the many young and old.
Stories of different cultures around.

But what I have learnt most is that Gua, Hua
and Dua became God's transitional prayers
which are centuries old.

All you need is God in spirit, never forget the
story of what this old man just told.

Portuguese Maritime Routes

In 1497 Manuel l asked Vasco da Gama
we need a trade route stop to help
us with some exchanges with India.

The fortification on the island became
a resting point.
Once fully occupied they returned
to Lisbon, laden with shiploads of gold.

When gold became limited,
Human labor became the new bold.

Fortification St. Laurent

Unpolluted In Our Spiritual Ways

Burma's virgin jungles.
One illnesses and its living
soils will consume you.

The jagged Arakan mountains,
scored by steep river valleys.

Burma's geographically critical point,
sea ways, and war strategic history.

The Pearl Harbour link.
Ping ponged between,
Japan and England continuously.

Burma's people the cleanest
of the clean, living on its golden lands.
Powered by its ancestral spirits
and the will of its people, oh
so grand.

They would always chant:

>   *The purple mountains the*
>   *vibrantly blue seas.*
>   *The wings covered some days*
>   *by foggy clouds.*

>   *Mentally connect us continuously*
>   *to the heavens.*
>   *The awakening of our souls.*

We don't mind visitors but we are
spiritually very unpolluted.
Please don't permanently stay,
unless you follow our holiest of ways.

A depiction of a holy shamanic
mountain and the core of earth.

-N-

The Beauty Of Raw

Indigenous you are,
your mountains of pain
called Kalahari.

Roots you pull,
for a handful of water.
Meat you steal from cheetahs.
Bush men,
You have a very raw
tribal beauty.

The land tells us
your part of humanities
earliest ancestry,
called the first clans of
earth.

Sing to the skies,
we can only wonder.
The vision of darkness,
in your path that
was once way past yonder.

The nights of no lights;
the cold with no heat.
How did you survive
natures horrible defeats?

Diagram Depiction of Bushmen

Don't You Ever Lose The Fight

Don't you ever, ever give up.
Even in your darkest moments
of the ocean's swell.
Ride that seven years of misery
known as the black side,
the yin's, incursion to the yang of hell.

Did you think an angel was
born without its counterpart.
Wear your tribal masks.
This is the normal combination
of our karmas of past life.

When the clouds of darkness hits.
And the mind has gone.
Run quick to a love one and
let them grip both your arms.
Don't you dare, scream through.
Make sure they also fiercely shake you.

A loving hand, can ward off anything
especially when an omen sends in its devil
after you.
Feel your beating heart,
our forefathers would once say.
As the blood rushes by,
these are the normal difficulties,
that everyone has to go through.

The design of life is simple it was
meant to confuse you.
Be understanding,
everyone struggles just like you.
There are no exceptions to this rule.

Don't you ever lose the fight.
A test of survival for the next.
Just remember we are all God's children,
and her spirit in the skies really does loves
you like the rest.

The Spawns of Hell

Mountains Of Pain

Heee- Mal-Aya we pray to you…

The skies, the spirts, the moons
of our very first.
What is the most important in
terms of spiritual beliefs,
we ask of you?

The after life, obviously!

Through their chants, the mighty
spirits would speak back.

> Erect you will do the special number.
> In shamanic belief the number seven,
> became a holy number of the ones that
> use to day by day consume you.

The seven groups of monuments
were erected.
A replica located in the valley
of death.

> Good! Its lethal peaks you wont need to
> pass through.

Katmandu represented the other point of
Hindi. The landing and earliest transposed
powers of the fiercest of them all.

The mountains, the seven temples and the
ones who can devour you. The light of birth
of devotion and that of our piety in terms of
highest powers.

Now became a cremation site and its earliest
shamanic beliefs will now be an idle for you.

Hi-Mal-Aya Mountains

Masters Of The Virgo

We are passionate fearless
forces of art.
Medieval, Tulips, Sadness
All play the part.

Low is our sea land
we shade in.
High are the peaks,
we colour paint.

The wind delicately moves the
windmills, these painters have
made with flowery shades.

Pain reflects the crosses of
designs.
The real life stories of
our past.
Filled with angelic divine.

The old the new, each
era of copycat artists,
their passage of time needed
to pass the wintery landscapes.

Art may be part of our spirits
but wine is the accessory to
help our imagination flow.

We have all become
"Masters Of The Virgo".

The Flightless Bird

Ancient flora and fauna,
a region known as heaven.
What happened to you Takahe?
Do you not wish to fly like the
rest of us?

Did God punish you in a past
life, that you can't look down
at those below you?
Join us we would say.

He answers back.

Ancient Gondwanaland were my forefather's
regions.
The divine blue falls, the gullies, the
mountains make me stay. Why would I leave
paradise and maybe fall prey?"

Leave me be, I simply prefer to stay.

Rare Flightless Takahe Bird

N6- New Zealand

Taumatawhakatangihangakoauauotamateapokaiwhenuakitanatahu hills are my home

The Mythical Land Whanganata

Ulu were once your holy mountains
that you would pilgrimage too.
Where do you go now,
Maori people?

We are brave,
But the numbers that come
can hurt us.
We have permanently settled in the outreach,
the smaller inlet of the two.

Your dances of fear,
and face all made up
in animal gear.
Do you fight back
Maori people?

No, they all smile.

We stick out our
warrior tongues,
and make lots of noises.
They then leave us
real quick.
This is our way.

We are known as the fearsome tribe.

Maori Warrior Sticking Out Tongue

N8- Nicaragua

Niiii They Screeched

Half naked they bend over to drink.
The moon glistens on the holy black lake
they called Nicaragua.
No different than God's water in India
Just 50,000 years earlier.

Niii they also use to screech!

Niii

N9- Niger

The Aga Of The Region

The Hausa people they would say:

Until the hunt is in favour of the lion,
the hunter or king will always be the lead
Aggg of its territory.

I travelled to India, where I live with my other African brothers who have lived in India for centuries, only to find out in there local Kannada languages they also would say:

Until the hunt is in favour of the lion,
the hunter or king will always be the lead
Aggg of its territory.

The Lead

White-Face Painted, African Tribe

Your color may be the same,
but you are from the other side.
Fierce is your battles.
Trust we have not.

Your appearance may be the same,
but you are from the other side.
Our language is different,
for our protection.

Your women we do crave,
but you are from the other side.
Come we take them and
kill you to pieces.

Your land is harsh but we can
still use, we never forget
you are from the other side.
Only one white face clan can
survive.

African brothers,
Ibo, Kanuri, Hausa, and
Yoruba tribes
are to mention the few.
We are merely ten minutes away,
yet we are not the same,
you are from the other side.

The Dancing Tribes

Negroid

Are you offended that
I call you the darkest of them all.

Picked violently from Chad, Niger, Sudan
on feces infested boats.
The blaring sun was your only
naked coat.

The house and the field
separated you,
the scars and battles
wounded you.

The fruits of the this
world made you sweet.
It was man that got confused
and try to make you weak!

Ill mannered is not
that bliss.
When we look at the
damages on our
historical list.

Are you offended that
I call you the darkest of them all.

Don't be, it is a replica of
Humanities ignorant mist.

Bedouin Indigenous Female

Clan female!
Decorate yourself so beautiful,
for our first night.

Always cover yourselves.
We have many men
from miles away
that can sense your
virginity.

Go get water in
groups.
We will protect you till death.

You carry the life of our
ancestry.
We know once they touch
you we would have lost our
forefathers.

Clan female!
Protecting you, means
protecting our genes,
that will carry us through.
Only we can touch you.

Bedouin Indigenous Female

Forested Shaman

In spirit do I see,
an outline of glass,
foggy white in nature.

Forested shaman
where do you hide?
Your bones are only
left in sacred sites.

Let your suckers of life,
come back through to us.
And now be the tips
of the tree tops.

Forested Shaman
Why do you howl to us?
Let your essence finally rest.
We will now connect with
you in spirit and nature.

Forested Shaman

Great Spirit In The Sky

Oh great ancestry,
we call on you.
The moon, the spirits, the earth.
We were born
free.

From the same mother.
Sacred is our rock,
pain is our rituals.

Oh great ancestry,
life is the soil under our feet.
Look at the sky.

Our connection will
always be to you.
Calls to you are made
to lead us to
the Hee's in the skies.

Shamanic we sing,
out to you!
Hiawatha now a leader,
of a great spirit.
We bow to you.

Where There Are Feathers, There
Were Shamans

We have officially healed,
we just wrote off humanity
and called it a day!

Healing

Man, Women And Child

The blood of a female
soaks into the moss,
between her private.

Picked delicately from the top of
stones, that harbour the moss.
It has always been pressed and
dried softy in
the shade known as heaven.

§

The child's excretion,
wiped outside with snow.
Its small body
becomes slightly frozen.

Until mother and child
are hidden under the
heavy leather caribou
tarp, the child keeps crying.

§

The man's wounds
an omen from a wild
animal's kick.

Healed with a birch and plant
mix.
Medicine a shaman doctor
has provided.

Man, women, child are the
        extension of earth.

The Circle Of Life

Blessings & Misfortunes

In a time of earthly devastation
what does one hand
say to another?
Come let me help you.
We are human in design.

In time of abundance
what does one hand
say to another?
Stay the way you are, and agonize.
This is self preservation.
We are still human in design.

The difference is simple
if you can see.
One is an omen collectively from the skies.
The other is internally coded in early
human creations.
Of the need to subdue and
the existence in beings.

Centuries old behaviours and
ancient are these encoded social
codes of genetics.

The key is breaking a perception
and what is better always for both
you and me.

The Human Bond

Once upon a time Koreans of common blood lived as clans in small groups; then their tribes got bigger.

Now their people are a homogenous race mixed with other Turkic, Mongolian and Tungustic (Tun-gush) people all belonging to the Altaic group of languages.

Yi Admiral Sun-sin

Darkness And Ice

Male is the land we walk on.
Blonde and giant we are.
Made fierce from the ice covered land.
Norse is the power that makes us
stand tall.

We tell the world,
we don't give a shit who's
forefathers we bear.
Animal was before us.
Made by God was each child
crafted and our own.

Compare us to no others,
we don't accept any.
Christian Scandinavian
centuries old,
is what was picked up.
Culture we ride with might.

We rise high and proud,
we are Norsemen till death,
may you tell the skies?

Norway's Outline

The Nor-Way Is The Path

Our first settlements by the
shore are dated at 5,000 B.C .
Germanic became the brothers
of our stock.
Comprised of Baltic, Alpine and Nordic.

Our clan were chieftains and warriors
different from the rest.
Our women so strong, even gave
birth in snow.
The matter of life, mixed with the blood of
cold.
Our first got moulded from our land, our
children of the snow.

Year after year our earliest indigenous
used raw hands on ice, to lumber or fish.
Tempted to live was our fight to exist.

The northern skies,
the Nor-way now became our
path of light,
This is exactly how we were born.
Our proud heritage past and what we
call our home.

The Northern Light

The 21 Tombs

In the early morning hours
one of our youngest was
sacrificed.

Hardship on the land was
the reason.
We were sure we had done
something wrong.

The eldest decreed death
to him.
Ghostly white was his colour
and we were sure the skies
would prevent omen once
they reaped all the benefits.

Our funeral practices are different
from others. We can only feed
them and place their bones after
seven moons, on the eve of sunset.

Beehive shaped is our graves and
the vengeance the skies cast on us
is dedicated to our females,
our monumental praying towers.
But first we sing:

> *Al Ayn chant again*
> *Al Ayn*
> *Al Ayn*

May spirit of the spirit return and bless
these lands and our steeple called Al
Khutm.

The 21 Tombs

-P-

The Kafirs Of Hindu Kush

By the Hunza river, how we prayed.
Animalist indigenous was our cliché.
Utler is our region, how the ones flying
control our ancient shamanic ways!

The British once overly enjoyed their
stay.
But so did the Greeks, Chinese, and
Persians

Beautiful are our women, the stories
of their lives alone can be made
into a historical essay.

Blue Eyed Brown Skin Child

The Regions Of Kashmir

Dark skin, blue eyes.
Native your people
still are.

A rare phenotype but this time
not distinct to one person.
Groups of them, makes these
people distinctive in style.

How beautiful these human are!
Even Alexander the Great once had
said.
> Carry a few females back home
> It's their piercing eyes
> some will be bred
> Our children they will store.

Kashmir was one territory of its original
people.
Uttar was the other.
The landing point are its pain riddled
mountains.
Ancient were there ways, they once freely
roamed.

One sect of our earliest humans
carrying blue eyes.
The earliest indigenous transformations
of permanent blues on earth.
Call them earths rarity, designed by the
heavens in its rarest form.
A n interesting genetic social display.

Why did the shark not eat the indigenous by Kayangel?

He knew the waters were abundant with fish and he could share.

The Cleaners of Our Seas

We Are First Clan

We are first clan
indigenous in nature.
Born on this land.
Living with the other brown Jews,
for centuries always offering a hand.

Out came the blonds
and attempted to assert
themselves on our holy lands.

They said something about an exodus,
that my friend is silly.
These were their summer homes.
Who merged with the few left after the
Holocaust but in reality Palestine
was ours to house the many.

The Answer

We are also first clan!
Do not be fooled by the
quick change over in colour.

Slavery dispelled us from our own
territories.
North Africa and the entire Anatolia
became the range of our earliest Jews.
Kazar's are what you must be
referring too?

For centuries we asked the sultans to
give us a small plot of land.
And then there are the many
archaeological finds,
that should be enough evidence there.
This was God's call, what he declared.

As for the Exodus this is true, are you dispelling
our will?
We laid the holy rock first,
this is our land, please do not mutter.

The Response

The land was not owned once upon
a time. Lies you do you are only Europeanized;
do you think we are fools?

We are no different, than the tragic tale of north
American Native too. For centuries we were here
with the original Jews.
We had an Ottoman neighbourly bond,
our saddest journey and woe became born
when it was gone.
What do you mean do not mutter?

The Answer

Fine think as you wish.
We came and took like others,
What do wish to do?

Palestine

Green Canopy Tops

Hanging off my balcony,
all I see are the green tree tops.
Living do they colour the skies,
screaming are the noises,
that come out of them.

My world is coloured,
like the vibrancy of colour in them.
Foggy and dew filled in design.
Hand painted from the heavens,
green are our canopy tree tops.

Gualaca Panama

The Lord Of The Flies

We march through the hardest
of swamp lands called Inanwatan.
We have no elders our tribes
are made up of predominantly many
young adolescents barely reaching
of age.

Ten thousand years ago,
our favourite foods were
banana and yam.

When others attack we fed
them to the skies.
But before we did, the leads
got the heart, we only got the hands.

The Soul Of An Enemy

Indigenous We Are

Potato Yucca and Yam
We crush with our feet.
Indigenous we are.
A love we have,
in sharing when we eat.

Mestizo, Ache, and Chiripa
is our local people.
The first on the land
that would speak.
Descendents of Guran.

Their spirits they would
recount of that in the sky,
that would always be watching
the harvesting season that went by.

Culture beyond the moons.
Is what we sing.
Home to our active
God Amamba,
the destruction of
what she can brings.

Indigenous we
are when we tap.
Help us compress
our starches for
our winter fest.

It helps the time
go by faster so we
can dance.

Potato, Yucca and Yam.
Watch us prance.

Guaran People

Peruvian

Spaniard you came,
so much blood,
on your hands.
You dressed us shut and
said we were not even a man.

Spaniard you forced.
Ancient skies were once our beliefs.
Suddenly a white man, blue eyes,
over time was the one
that gave us relief.

Battles so fierce,
we quietly knew you had won.
But something happened
an irony of the past gun.

We merged old with new,
one generation after another.
More like 500 years later.
This was a part of history's funny
manoeuvre.

Today even if we wanted to go
back, we would fight you violently!

Spanish nights became our
Peruvian style.
Feverishly colourful in design
was now our flavour for
everyone to see.

Spanish-mix indigenous,
became our forefathers evolved.
Grown from our historical wounds,
an emergence of culture with love.

We personally don't focus about the ethics
of past, in all this jive.
A heart which burst through our shirt can now
be seen, that Hispanic today has become our
national pride.

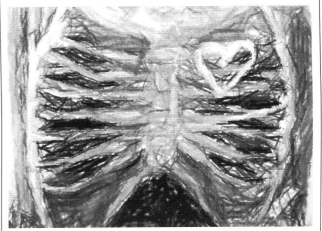

The Flaming Heart

Nonbeliever

Let's discuss the difference
between a nonbeliever and one
that magnifies God's name.

Nonbeliever, accept all oblations since
God had to have given existence,
and therefore judges all truth.

You know all the moral,
Palawan long, Marianna trench deep
kind of stuff.

The one closest to hell,
that carries immense depth.
That doesnt scare you.

Nonbeliever, does this bore you?
Probably so, but ironically
only in despair, when your pain is
unbearable and your darkest anguish
comes to light.

Do you ignore your thoughts of reason,
and scream out for anything that
could be a saviour.

Nonbeliever, offer what he abominates.
Heal yourself with what the skies
and the energies of what the cosmos
has to offer you.

One-day morality and judgment may
reincarnate you.
My advice to you, don't take chances.
Since being balance, or that of
equilibrium, are the laws

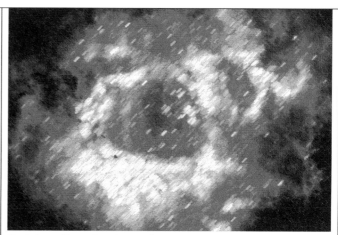

Spirituality And Faith

of all the universes.

P10- Poland

The Churches Of Peace

The significance of the basis of morality.
What if I told you God exists, would you
be morally correct?
What if I told you God doesn't exist,
would you be morally correct?

Philosophical as it may sound the
question to humans then becomes:
Should we or shouldn't we think,
to be socially and morally correct?

The basis of morality therefore shouldn't
be dependent on that of the possibility of
the
questions of God.

Entrenched into ideology of centuries old,
Jawor, the invading armies to the pagan
people
of the region would say, do you actually
question honour and the skies?

Remember the revelation of angels
dictates a real examination of the one
above.

Faith

Boats in the harbour 1830.
Long dangers of voyage
to new exotic places.
Fado recite to us history about
the sadness of our early voyage,
missing home and
their longing for their comfort places.

Socialist reforms and
radical propaganda
became Lisbon's darkest censorship.
Fado tell us a political story about
what was done in 1929.

Folk dances, long dresses.
Catholicism push to heal.
Fado sing to us your old
rural songs of saddens, romance,
cultural heritage.
An entire nation struggles and
tunes of different human ordeal.

The epoch has entered 2000 and they
are still proud Fado singing
Portuguesismo.

-Q-

The Royal Tribe, Bani Tamim

The Portuguese in the 1500's were the worst, to our earliest people in Catara. An attempt to make a fortification failed horribly.

Then came the migrating Al Khalifah people in the 18th century who started relocating to North western Qatar, the Persian's immediately felt threaten and invaded it stationing troops in the region.

We were actually happy under Persian rule because they accepted our local people's names of shamanic beliefs and even intermixed with us. They also taught us honour. We were only one tribe of family then of approximately 50,000 people.

In 1914 the British during Ottoman came and created a treaty that sheltered us as a protected state.

It took several years but thank God we gained our own liberation in 1971. The virtue of freedom gave us the blessing of an independent state.

-R-

R1- Romania

Drakula

We are the first.
Seven represents our holy
number of death.

We cut its throat let it bleed
and drink to be men.
A form of aphrodisiac by the entire
tribe.

This has been the core of shamanic
living since way back then.

Dracula

Our seven villages inscribed and
founded by the Transylvanian Saxons
 has existed since Middle Ages.
We make sure all our churches are
 in fortress format.

Our legend today still rings through as
the one
who drinks blood.

A Goblet of Blood

R2- Romania

Bucharest is our capital today, but hear
he.
To the beauty of the skies, we also once
use to fly.

Catherine The Great

Many lovers do I have.
A symbolism of force.
A Europeanize heritage I
gave to Russia.

Make love do I do,
to broker a peace treaty with
the Ottomans.
The year is now 1774.

Annex our land we make up.
Split our land we separate 1787.
A circle now designed by an enemy's mate.

Let's try this again my lover that I enjoy.
Flamboyant I am, you are my toy.
Annex our land we make up.
Split our land, one final clash,
before we forever go 1792.

Russia needs a foothold in
the black sea my advisors
are told.
Austria is also our enemy,
the Crimean Peninsula,
in a position so bold.

Build up the navy
in the greatest of way.
For the towns and small cities.
Russia will now forever stay.

Livid I am at their Ottoman Empire,
I have no mercy.
Loyalty they want from me,
but promiscuous are my curvy tools.
Catherine the Great I am, they
must be totally confused.
They want me tame,
like an animal locked in a zoo.

Who the hell are these
clans, unlike others.
They are socially funny in design
watch them pray.
I won't sin with an opposing other.

They will learn the hard way
at my inner strength,
I will defeat their armies and show them
I am no damn fool!

Catherine The Great

R4- Russia

Out of this chaos emerged Russia, whose victories at Khazan freed their country of their Tatars dominations.

One to One…did they battle

Different Tribe / Same Battle

R5- Russia

The Passageway Of Energy

Large masses of energy once past through God's hand on earth.
A few Venus' he laid claim,
to breed.
The shamanic might
of first women.
The drawings of life
hidden in a Denisova Cave.
They are our females,
to think about.
They were called the
Mother's of earth for
a reason.
Energy is the spirit they
gave to each head of
clan that roamed;
in the darkness of the
vast plains.
Feeding the spirits through
their breast,
became their magnificent
capacity for existence.
The energy channel of life
from one soul to another.

Atomic Power Of The Universe

The Circle Of Life

The lengthy migration has halted.
The hundreds of reindeers on this
vast green plain now simply
circle continuously.

Even the token rare white
one, looks so well blended in.
Our special spirit, the Natives
once would say.

A large buck, would be our eye
marker in following the full rotation
of this circular motion.
Viewing them on top of the plains.

Man needs not look
at sciences but rather what
our own surroundings give us
in terms of information.

Chemicals they spew continuously
not realizing in the end all of it goes
back to the basics.

This circle of life.

Our earliest forefathers would
study the variety of
magnetic pulls of earth.

No different than the irony of this
herd and a single white buck twirling
around in a daze.

They would attempt to make
sense of the world they lived
in then.
A prayer of blessing of what is
indigenous and their traditional
knowledge's past on today.

The Prayer of Indigenous Traditional Knowledge.

Fierce Child

Hands so small,
yet dry blood is filled
under your nails.

When you should be
really playing with toys.
Lost in the confusion
of the scars you bear.

The omen of social
ills brought forth
from primitive man.

Ripped becomes
your tiniest body.
Amongst men
that man you.

Fierce child,
forgive humanity
for not protecting you
today.

Dedicated to children soldiers.

-S-

The Drastic Mistake Of Early Man

Dead today, your lush forests are now gone.
Once home to an infestation of hominids.
Lively were your animals in the streams.
Oh Sahara how much damage has our
earliest people of earth done?

Variety of creature's in disguise,
from tree to tree. Continuous water vapour,
a splendour of mist to see.
Multitude of colour was what housed
the spectrum of rainbows because
of the life it stored.
Called the compost breathing on dead clay
grounds, and treetop singing sparrows.

Then primitives, slowly but truly
transformed this land.
Humans now became the display of earth.
The dominant start of settlement and that of
early man.
An attempt to cultivate the arid terrain.
The failure of soil became our horrid
disarray.

In all of our history, nothing was fiercer
than then the pulling of life from the land.
An intricate underground network,
called the vital component of earth.
The dead now became our inherent and
continuous environmental battle, the
gradual transformation to an arid
wasteland.
It all started with domesticated animals, the
source of food and the extra helping hand.
Animals were used to remove the roots
called the suckers, the living beneath the
land. Roots of bushes were dried and laid.
Trees eventually started to fade away.

Our first heating became the only way.
Chocked became vegetation, the tiniest became
the pockets that stayed.

Battle of forces to what dwindled,
a drastic mistake of earth was clearly made.

Listen to these words carefully of what our
primitives would once say. There are 900
million square miles, look for land, and fire
fuel Sah-ara (Sağara).
This was our earliest struggles and shamanic
ways.
The first words of our forefather's whispers a
completely different story for us today.

Over time reminiscent of everything living on
its soil disappeared. Swallowed and broken up
by the breakables. Called the fluctuating
weather and harsh tumbler sands.
Compounded heat grew, now became the
tumour of our ancestral lands.

Man now looked for alternatives. The black-
shale in earth's cracks moved from second to
first in command.

Mother earth damaged nothing left over to
last.
Dead became the region, it changed all our
maps.

Sahara Desert

Caribs

When visited by Christopher Columbus he said "the Caribs are warlike and cannibalistic in nature. We need to humanize them. I will name this Island after one of the fourteen holy helpers. Sankt Christopher, the Patron Saint."

The seas are rugged we get violently
green and sick.
When at night we go to sleep,
Fourteen angels watch over us.
Two my head are guarding,
Two my feet are guiding;
Two upon my right hand,
Two upon my left hand.
Two who warmly cover
Two who o'er me hover,
Two to whom 'tis given
To guide our steps to heaven.

We will pray.

The Caribs

The Volcanoes That Spoke

Look inside,
the Piton's are hungry.
Throw one more in.

If you madden them
they will spit immense heat.
Stay very still
and pray to them.

They are our faceless men.
Their anger makes us
steer clear, only when we suffer
we know its time to feed.
Oh the brew-ha of mayhem.

The medicine man in the tribe
is the only one who can see them.
The rodents and opossums we also
feed them.

Watch them produce the white heat.

Soufriere, St Lucia Volcanoes

Amerindian Worship

We have found an altar which shows worship on the island.

We are able to communicate with them.

They say their lives depended on the great spirits from above, and that they prayed in secret each sunrise.

They told us a story about why they held a polished black rock in their hands.

The idea that they can be strong like the sacred black rock.

The Blessed Black Polish Rock

Tutuila

We sing to the skies,
for we were all ocean born.

We pray to the heavens
for our land teaches us
the skies merciless blows.

We dance around our dead
for they will come back
as spirits untold.

Ut Ut, Ulu or Ula the father,
ghost and Holy son prayers our
earliest shamans globally told.

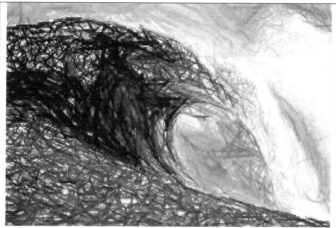

Region Pago Pago, Samoa

Ave Maria

The sounds, our surroundings once
bestowed to our humans.
They included the start of
refine words and beautiful tunes.

Ut, re, mi, fa, sol, la; Ti and Do

We were against the reformation
to our heavenly Gods.
Our idols and sacrifices to him we did
love.
We sang to him, please help us and
destroys all our foes.

Did it work, oh no.

We built on top of this mountain, the
mighty Titan. A castle protective and so
bold.
We started creating art, literature and
now composed
today it became...

Do re mi fa so la ti and doe

Our Sky Was Once Owned By The First
People Of Earth.

The Land Made Me

I am a chameleon, evolved from the land.
I see therefore my internal just picks up
the many colours of my surrounding.

This is called germination and the by-
products of what was given from the
land.

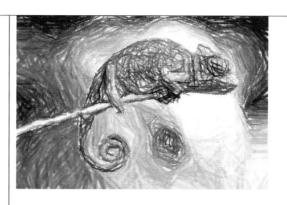

We Apologize

In more recent times,
Ottomans did we hate.
But let not for-take,
The reason or
the missing component of
our historical awake.

When those shamans
needed written,
it was our alphabet,
that they raked.

They spread it across
North Africa to Iran.
And did not offer grace.
They called us primitive
thus little is known.

So much history and
differences we have.
That which was written
in stone.

Yes we are different
and do marry,
One, two, three and sometimes four.
This is part of our past, an
indigenous protective score.

Misunderstood by the foreign.
Who are always welcome to stay
but don't even bother or come near.
All of our females are fully owned,
even in the present day.

Today we are shocked to learn when
Rih-yad became our earliest spirits.
Yanbu, Karan, and Dalgan
became a loan.

We apologize to the ancestries
of Ottomans for the hotel
we just made of their
old homes.

Cultural heritage will now be
part of our protected zones.

Al-Alyad Ottoman Fort

In the Battle of Life

Aryan men were designed
from a miniscule speck,
in the spectrum of multitude of colours.
A single molecule,
copied an encoded light.

God's gift to the colour charts.
Purity white in sheer delight.

They too were part of them,
way back then,
in the battle for life.

Not aware in the past,
other colours diluted
each era to the next.

One day a holy apple was
given to a she which,
is now their permanent might.
Today education became,
the supreme, our power of fight.

The key is their genetics
were always there.
Our Aryans, their rare
colour white was
a gift from the very start of life.

The Opposite Spectrums Of Colours
and Life

In the Battle of Life

A seed from under earth,
the breaking of soil, our first female.
Became an extension of primary life.
Designed, from the skies onto the womb,
she became "mother first".

An indiscriminate random pick,
in the multitude of colours.
A single molecule of colour,
was picked from the heavenly skies.

This was God's will, a colour
chosen from the charts.
The earliest browns,
now became our sheer delight.

Those that followed inherited
a piece of them, way back then,
this was one part in the
battle for life.

Not aware in the past,
other shades also called the
first colours of earth,
mixed in and diluted,
each era to the next.

These dominants now became
the first clans of earth.
Shaman became thy name.
Roamed for millions of years
In the hunt for game.

The key is their genetics
were always there.
Our almondy browns were
a gift from God, our dominant hues
from the very start of life.

Dances of Life

Resistance is futile
they told the tribes
along the Senegal river.

We clash fiercely
dances till death.
Ululate we called on others.
All alone were we in
the battle during slavery.

Shaman straw dresses.
Foreigners we battle and
felt no mercy,
when we ripped.

Not a bone in our body
for you to catch.
Just a song or two.
To celebrate their defeat.

Famous are our Senegalese
dancers from the very start.
Our leads dressed up
with a mask and a heart.

Try catching us, we will
two-step around you.
We do the dances of life,
and we are not kidding when
we say that to you.

The Seven Ethnic Groups Of
Senegal

Stari Ras

Deep in the human
psyche, a horrid
weakness exist.

One of fear,
the very human
need to be dominated.
A collection of weight.
That makes the soul
obsessed.

Controlled becomes
our spirits.
Lack of power in
our thoughts is now
our weakness.

Free yourself!
God whispers,
and ease your internal
from all the negative
spirits.

The King of all Hawks,
Uros in 1260 built
these monuments that will
be here to help protect
 you always.

King Uros

We land here it is1609. In this region that I feel is like the Garden of Eden,

I declare there has to be a God!

British East Indian Company Expedition

Raven's In The Sky

I carve this ivory stone,
that looks like
a raven.

I think of only one thing
as an African man we posses
one power others don't.
Our impenetrable will.

Raven we call out to you.
You give us our strength.

The pursuit begins.
We follow you so you can
let us know where the water
hole is.
Our hunt for food and some
deerskin.

Remember our impenetrable will.
Oh what songs we will sing.

The Raven Made From Ivory

My Motto Is Balance

In a world so hard
democracy, peace, progress,
justice and equality
is what I ask for.

But when I have a fair
country should there
be actually more?

The eye in the sky
to the depths of hell.
Reciprocal, up and down,
the emotions of our lives
go?

The tightrope walk
is my goal
while keeping a
balanced load.

In my lowest points,
what would life be?
I reach back high to
attain as I try to cope.

In my highest point,
what would life be?
I try to refrain, and instead come
down to enjoy the smaller
tingle of joy.

My motto is balance
as I walk this tightrope.
*But once was written in very ancient Javanese
language form. Cited in a different ritual.
Lord Save us, he is the one I pay homage,
in present invisible form.*

*At the focus of any meditation to heal the
soul will be embodied in both the material and
immaterial wealth of existence from the land
we were born*
.

You will provide the great calm.

Kulamun Durung lugu
Aja pisan dadi ngaku- aku.

Balance

Our Indian Prince

Centuries ago the people of Malay once said,

Utama is what we should be looking in the skies for.

Our prayers were heard.

The skies then produced a son and he now came to us as the first person of earth in human form.

They called the first in the region born an Indian Prince.

Indian Prince Sang Nila Utama

Is There A God?

Oh skies above
is there a God?

Does he exist
and if there is,
who made God?

The answer is:
Universe to Universe,
Star to Star,
Demän to Demänovska,

Even the underground
world, with its hot-cold caverns
of dark, were built
by the hand of dusted gold.

With the speck of first
stone put by divinity of the
supreme.

Therefore, we enlighten
the many.

Even the God's
had to have had a God
from before.

The Demon In The Karst Cave

The Stilt Houses Of Slovenia

Seven thousands years ago,
at the edge of the rivers or the lakes.
Man left us marks of our early prehistoric
keepsakes.

Glacial was the temperatures with barely
any sleight.
Social development is the highlight of
how advanced our earliest made way.

Our European Prehistoric Villages

Darkness

Don't go too deep,
the water is dangerous.
Its suction will pull you in.

It living soul will not protect you.
Instead ride the tides,
in the mornings you will
heal yourself.

And don't go too deep.
There in the darkness
he that rises.

The Darkness In The Tide

Shaman You Are, Shaman I am

Its two years and we have made it to the tributaries. Tired we are.

What you speak and I speak are relatively constant. This was the case of what came out of our animal world.

When phonetics and dialects were the only
variations. No different than the monkey's in
the trees.

Shaman its now 50,000BC! Why are you completely changing?
the order of your first sentences or words?

Are you protecting your own clan from our destructive tribes that have started to hunt you in this breeze?

Hominid Dialogues

In the Light Of The Sun

We called our kings Kral,
the Dutch made it cattle!

Our name of shamanic belief
was San, the British turn us
into wild Bushmen.

Our land was free.
The diamonds and gold rush
in the late 1800's
eventually made our own territory
into the Queen's land.

We wanted to break free of Apartheid
but they put our leader into the horrid
pen.

When in reality, if we listen to the
wounds of the earth we were born as
the leads of all of the land.

The Shamanic Sun

Many Moons Ago

Once upon a time
humans were all brothers.
In an inlet place they said
proto-Turkic in its advanced
linguistic form was born.
The first marks of life
on the oracle of bones.
This was before the 1400's
time zone.

To Korea many went.
History in search of.
Only to find Hangul's
three kingdoms
were hidden in full dialogues,
pre-enlightenment to the world.

We are the ancient people,
who worship the suns and embrace
the moons.
Let go of your animal kingdom
strife and let the planet bloom.

World powers said no!
Two thousand years ago when these
institutions were set up we couldn't change
these administration point of views.
And yes we did know.

Their books of hundreds of years now
overthrown. We never focused on unwritten
and their linguistic change overs,
to be honest shaman is still very new to us
and unknown.
We do feel very low.
Today Korea proudly says:
Humanity has done such a
defeat.
Progress is understanding
what is global history.

The migratory dialogues of our earliest
and its two million years of
55,000 people's shamanic ancestry.

We celebrate, the skies, the earth
And what it means to just be.....

May the world release doves for global peace.

S23- South Sudan

Once upon a time, more like over 10,000 years ago. Our land was lush, green and full of water.	

S24- Spain

The Sons Of Darkness

Spain spoke:

*Sons of darkness some of your other
clans must be.
Hebrew is also your ancient alphabet.
Salamanca is your regional dialects.
But why is your beliefs of birds something
you refuse to let go?*

What is your choice they continue on and say: Death, or expulsion?

To the highest courts we make a command we will simply do a forced conversion, something for us that is so delightfully grand!

Christ is our saviour,
to the Yahud believing Jews.
Our churches will now
depict you as a gargoyle.

While the Christian mercenaries
of light peck at your skull
in the hells of fire.
Learn from us the right way.

Today we ask you Spain
tell us the real truth,
behind how recent was
the length of time
to transfer to a monotheistic God?

One of a hidden whispering campaign.

Ci or Si or Sea?

Which Si was meant to be?

Somewhere in a cave
in the coldest point of
the world, early humans
looked for si.

But not the sea they
would like it to be!
In migration they moved to
Siberia, known first as si leri.
By the waters edge in our
Shu-man-ik history.
But this was not the si either,
they would like it to be!

Many died, the ones that
travelled made it.
Hunter gathers
they still moved.
Our earliest first, wandered,
relocated to less
harsh lands.

People of Cieza (Ci-eza)
they became known.
Where their Sea,
the Spanish Si's became
their right Ci.

Holly fresh spring water was this Ci,
lined in order, all hearts open to the sky.
Their Roman fort, became strong,
by the sea.

Centuries later,
It provided us the clues,
to which
Ci or Si or Sea was the
people of Cieza's preference for Ci.

City of Cieza Spain

Columbus Said

I do not get it.
From East to West.
All I see are
barbaric shamans,
your highness.

How did they migrate
to both lands?
So many Indians I see!
From what I know
Kan-Tan are their
territories,
Kana are some of their people.

These are the first.
But there seems to
be many more.
We have killed
a few dozen.
And extracted a lot,
but we need men.
Lots of men.

Slavery did not work
well with them.
We now eye Africa instead,
we will build and dominate.
Like our forefathers before.

Your highness
if we don't,
we will starve here.
Our people are ghostly white.
We have no heat,
our land is not right

Please give us more
aid.
And lets take over
with full might.

Columbus And Spanish Queen

The Flying Goddess

Thanusha, or mighty one you were born
deep in the heart of Africa,
centuries ago.
Something rattled your spirits.
You travelled all the way
to Sri Lanka.

The land of cattle and Sigir,
our animals of richness and
divine traits.
Do you want to join in?

We have many Gods we
pray too.
What is one more of worship
I ask of you?

The flying Goddess continues
to sweeps around the skies.
You did not answer our
calls.
We ask you again Thanusha!

Maybe we will feed you quick and
run from you.

*"We know you can awaken all life. The power
to create hurricanes or stir all creatures that
have feet, and even make the other birds of air
fly up".*

Tan usha, don't use your might.

We will always acknowledge that you are
holy and great.

Our Goddess in the skies.

The land of cattle and sigir

They Asked Nubia?

What is the one thing you can't change
they
asked the many in Napatan?

The Meroitic speaking from Kushite
civilization
responded.

The Nubian order of life.
Don't try to accumulate wealth.

You will never win.
These other rulers in the surrounding
territories
are also large and very parasitic.
And don't want you there.

Stay a humble servant and chattel.
Instead focus on your quality of life.
Don't fall a slave, yet stay simple.
Prioritize your families' chores.

You come to this earth to be our
Kingdom's toy.

S29-Suriname

The Lieutenant for the Dutch West India Company said:

The Chinese blacks and the Bosch negroes are not integrating well, see if you can kill some men and intermix their women.

The depiction of real historical slave life, driven by those in power, had once said.

The Intermixing of slaves

S30-Swaziland

The Great River Of Usutu

They have killed or taken many mainlanders.
The people from the region of Sena near Zambezi river are now currently moving in.

Happy the land is now temporarily free of the other fractioning tribes.

Many artefacts like pottery and iron, from their homes can still be found.

The Sena locals said we are very confused though, why are these demons calling our peaks, a river now?

Make you Laugh Some More

One, two, three or four, I want to make
you smile
some more.

*Are you
Black,*
    *Are you
    Turkic,
    Are you
    Native,*
*I asked? These are the ancestral first of our
past!*

You must be ill, some Swedes said.
Our monkeys, Neanderthal in type
were bright white and fluffy.
Mix in the intellectual ferment,
genetic purity, is what we carry.
With baby blue eyes of
saturated light.

A quick response came
blaring through,
read this secret research.
What is a human clan,
and now understand the marry.
Educated on DNA ethics is the way,
all of humanity should now be.
    *Are you Black,
    Are you Turkic,
    Are you Native,
    I re-asked?*

Redeem yourself Europe for your craziest past!
Blankly, they quietly looked.
From something called shamans, and not a
stork or Vikings? Today we have become
even more confused?

Quick get the scholars to divert this horrid
mess. Some of us Swedes are now under
major distressed. Two days later this was
their very
polite address:

The land, filled with snow, made our skins
white like china,
the azure of the sea made our eyes
brightest of blues,
blonde was the sun converting our hair,
How dare you disrespect centuries of our
generational pool.

A huge smile was sent
to their height's above.
Don't be mad please.
This is exactly how I
gently tease!

The concept of being one,
as humans.
Theories on evolution,
whose monkey is better,
What is colour saturation
has humanity all in tears.

Love thy neighbour
laugh some more.
And don't be like others,
from colonial days who simply
wants a score.

Sweden's Christmases

Snow trickles down lightly.
Fireplace burning apple
scents so slowly.
All the mugs painted carefully.
Lil Peter joyfully says:

Papa open the calendar,
let's eat one more chocolate.
Tell me how many
more days till Christmas.

Eighteen more days
Don't let the pine
hurt your small hands.
Help me son lift this tree.

Grand mama open the calendar,
let's eat one more chocolate.
Tell me how many
more days till Christmas.

Fourteen more days.
Don't get that impatience.
Instead help stitch each popcorn
kernel.
Delicately around it goes in the
circle.

Mama open the calendar,
let's eat one more chocolate.
Tell me how many
more days till Christmas.

Seven more days.
All the glass
ornaments are up.
Help put the shimmery
sparkles, use the step stool
to get to the ones on top.

Grand papa open the calendar,
let's eat one more chocolate.
Tell me how many
more days till Christmas.

Tomorrow sweet child!
Don't peak at the gifts.
Patience is the key,
instead light all the candle tips.

Put the last socker around,
A little more time and then it becomes
another year gone.

Dedicated To Human

There comes a time when humanity has to understand the simplicity factor of the earth we live in.

All the technology of the world has zero value if we don't have the need internally to convert and coexist at peace. Even a corporate scaling back may be needed.

Thousands of years ago like your forefathers from before, they would once hold their hands to their many Gods in the skies.
This was the start, called the dawning of consciousness.

We too will one day raise our hands up to skies.
The spirit of Kanat and betterment merged together is the birth of higher reasoning.
An accession of the ills of past flights gone by.
Dear God,

We will live humbly and at peace with our environments only to survive, and not try to amass anything.

We will all be educated and avoid primacy at the highest levels.
And acknowledge we may be bored.

Every living person will kneel to the laws of earth implemented as designed. That the laws of earth for all are supreme, a global bonding to just be better.

We will more effectively communicate the problems of land. And give our women birth control. While putting a value on human life.

But most important we will acknowledge earth; it being our temporary holding cell and the signs to the skies on human rights day will read:

God we wish to boycott, sit and wait out this transition. A solemn pledge of brotherhood, how the thin shell of blood that you designed became human in spirit, how our world has agreed to become socially one for betterment now!

Human Rights Centre Geneva

Alp Is Still Thy Name

The green treetops produce dew.
Lethal are its peaks, thus
Alp became thy name.

"*You are the mountain warrior*",
us shamans once said.
For the many who lost lives
and the evil spirits you brought.
Even Asia couldn't touch your peaks.

Today so modern and pretty,
thousands of years later.
Geneva became their heart,
church bells replaced indigenous temples.
Many things have transformed.
Its people, its culture, its food.

One thing has not changed.
The green treetops still produce dew.
The mist of past settles on the
busy cities.

But Alp is still thy name.

Church By The Mountain

S35- Syria

One thousand years ago after a sacrifice was made, the wish for betterment and healing was done by praying to the Sky Gods.

Today we know better, that God just lets us be....

Hope

S36- Syria

The Shamans of Su'Riyah

We the Akkad's emerged from Syria. Much of our tribes were killed, our settlements
were brutally destroyed.

Now we became the Akkads of the Sumer regions. Caspian our new territory and home.

Our Semitic lead Sargon I was the one in control.
The Tigris and Euphrates is the holy water we still enjoy.

Sargon I

-T-

T1- Taiwan

Ilha Formosa – The Beautiful Island

We are the Malayo-Polynesian ancestry
of the aboriginal population of Taiwan.

The following people have all lived on
our island, the Portuguese, Han Chinese,
Dutch, Spanish and Manchua Asians.

Our forefathers would say…

Hell is frightening, with the souls of the
monstrous demons that exist.
Learn to always live at peace with the
ones who come and stay.

The Flowers Of Taiwan

T2- Tajikstan

Tadzhik

We are the ancient people of Sogdians.
We have lived in these dense river
networks for centuries.

From the outside we all look the same but
even our own tribe can be subdivided
into seven very distinct groups of people.

Most don't know but Sarazm is one of the
earliest proto-urbanization trade areas of
the region. Why do you need to know
this because our elders would say:

*We have seen many faces, heard many stories
but our ancestral bones still rattle in the sun,
today.*

Our Ancestral People

Tan Tan Goes The Gods

Tan Tan the noises of lightening
goes the Gods,
mortified when they strike down.

Ban Ban is the food
that we feed them,
hoping they don't prey on us.

On On is the ten fingers in the skies
is our destined plight,
their weight heavy.

Tar Tar is the hail,
under the moon,
their spirits above us.

Always remembering the murmurs
of puffy clouds.
That we all came from indigenous
known as the headless discarnate beings.

Hit cover quick, when Tan Tan goes
the Gods.

Lightening And Noise Of Tan Tan Goes
The Gods

Spirits Of Past Life

Two thousand years ago the Caucasoid people from Southern Kushite Ethiopia moved into our land. Our tribal pressures began.

At around the same time the iron wielding
Bantu people from Western Africa also moved in. They proudly eliminated most of our local tribes.

Everything was fine until the Portuguese came.

We then knew their spirited omens of our past ancestry had come back to cause havoc on the land.

Our people told the remaining part of them, it is because of your past actioms that tan tan now goes the Gods.

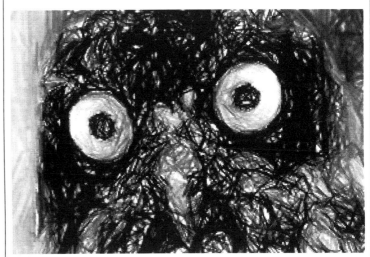

Mask Of Caucasoid Kushite People

Buddhism

Calm is our soul,
tranquility we find in nature.

We say to those lost,
put your hand in the mud and
feel the life in it.

Pick up the tiny worm,
in the mush of clay
and sense its soul move around.

Don't be disconnected
with earth.
That man made mounds of
concrete there to fool us.

Watch the life still move around,
It has a soul and a purpose,
understand the life within it.

We believe in a no kill policy for life.
The splendours of earth,
meant to connect us to human
from the divine.

Inside our homes.
We live with the bugs, scorpions and snakes.
Gently moving them from our paths.
Do you find our ways odd?

Your foods are that modified!
Your meat is packaged, hidden is
the torment to animal.
Heavy chemicals you use,
did you think they just disappeared?

They only come back to you
as a punishment from the skies.
Ironically we find your lack of quality
in life odd.

Mediate and understand earth
to feel linked to the skies.
It will heal you from the karma,
of injuring your own selves' in this cycle of
life.

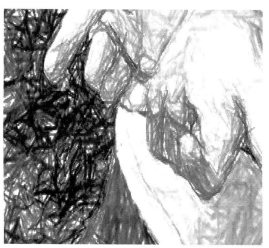

Child Holding worm

T6- Timor Leste

The Black Triangle

The power of many will crush any stupidity,
clans we will stay.

Let's battle these foreign and make them all go
away.

The black is the past omen of colonization;
the stars represent world peace at present day.

Heritage Symbols

T7- Togo

The Constant Of Vocal

Today we have literature, Ballet African du Togo and Art. But our forefathers once had said.

*Change is the only constant of the planet!
Albert Einstein would understand the Kwa people's musical dialogues better today.*

Eeee = mc ^{2}

Two Million Years Ago We Made Way

The Summit Of Volcano

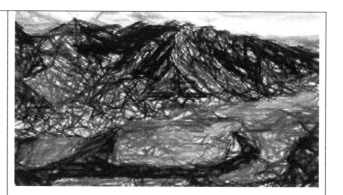

Our rituals for the preparation of war are an
actual process.
Our men are blessed in tapa cloth made of bark
and weave.

We must first drink the K'ava pepper plant
with its mild narcotic.
Once at the summit of the Volcano, they
have to feed the female bitch in the sky.

Help us sing this tribal chant.

maʻuluʻulu, maʻuluʻulu,

How we would pray as we told them
good-bye.

Young Coconut Jelly

Take the stone and crack
open the young coconut.
Drink its water and start
scooping out its mushy jelly.
Enjoy it slowly and heal your
brittle lips.

Then come join us,
darker skin you are.
Indian a lot of us are.

Trash bins we have made into
steel drums.
Day and night we beat on
to forget the impacts of
slavery and our own misery.

Now dance!
If you are still sad we may
put a little of the master's rum
in your jelly.

The Amphitheatre

Our elder has summoned
everyone!
He says this young man
is evil, at the first rainfall we
will sacrifice him.

Do not eat the poisonous plants.
You must feel the torment
otherwise the omen spirits
in you, will follow us back.

He died slowly screeching in pain.

His spirit from past life
returns to the very same spot
he was sacrificed.

This time the Romans are here.
They have replaced the
awkward stones.
And have opted to forgo this
shamanic site with
what looks like a colossal
structure.

They have name it the same though!
El-Jem is this structure's name.
For the laws of the first of the many
before them.
The only thing different other than the
size are the cages and what is
eaten today by lions.

It seems to be entertainment of
what was once done but in a more
advance way.

El Jem Amphitheatre

Hagia Sohia

A simple stone dolmen,
then a shamanic temple,
A church, today,
a transformed Mosque.

How you stand unbroken.
Magnificent is your splendour.
A renaissance of each era.

Aya Op Hi (hee)
When grunts were heard.
Did you wonder,
where their spirits went?
Or what was in the skies?

Saint Sohia
When Byzantium
church bells rang,
Did you hear the
howls of your earliest
forefathers?
The ones whose echo came
 from the skies.

Aya Sofya
When songs of
Ottoman prayers
blared out on,
Ramadan day.
Did you hear,
the church bells chime
of our past.

Hagia Sohia I ask of you:
Who came, who left?
Reminiscent of our past.
Your ancient structure.
Sprits of time,
concepts of the many Gods.
Who have disappeared over time.

So much blood,
Yet we are one generation
to the next,
just a humble passage of time.

In our indigenous hearts,
you will still be,
our ancient shamanic heritage.
Holy in wisdom
Aya Op he'ya

You stood the strongest test of time.

Christ In Hagia Sophia Today- The Moon And
The Spirits Aya Op Hi(hee)

The Hidden Underground

Derin Kuyu you are not the
only hidden.
Babel we cried out loud.
Don't fool us Gods,
anymore.

Oh lord, the damages we have
not knowingly done.
A million years of shamanic spoken
ancestry,
Holy in nature.
No more.

The written destroyed.
Past civilizations, and the lives
we harmed
No more.

Our hidden scripts, our ancestry
we now know.

Diagram is Derin Kuyu Turkey (Hidden
Underground City)

Istanbul

Find torment, our battles ensued. During bloody
clashes the ambassador in Constantinople was committed to the prison of the seven towers.

The seven became his lethal transposition of death. An omen that meant torture or consumption of what is afterlife.

London, United Kingdom

We are civil not like them. Evolve is our spirit. Even our dead will be delicately woven into our landscapes.

Today we will abandon the past and simply call our graveyards the "Magnificent Seven".

A Gravestone At Nunhead, One Of The "Magnificent Seven" London Cemeteries.

The Victims, Of The End Of War

Priest, I am so young with two small
children, they killed my husband.
We are Assyrian and this holy church is the
only thing I trust.
A boy can save himself.
I am going to Syria to find my
distant relatives.

Please can you just take my son
Till I can get him back.

The Priest responds:
We don't really have a lot but this is a house
of God, we will try our best.

Distant relatives, I am so young with a
single daughter.
The age of her breast are so tender please can
you take her,
till I get back.

If a few other days go by,
you can marry her to anyone.
A very sad day for me, for the clan violence
that may occur to a foreign child alone with
them.

This was our horrid family's faith.
Could this be better than death, I am
desperate. May she immediately produce a
son to ease her wounds, to blend in with
them.

God in this remote Assyrian church I stand
alone in front of you.
Can you forgive me for the life I am
about to take.
You know the forbidden in our cultures.

I don't know how to read or write.
My husband is the only man who should
touch the divine.
My kids she wails; this was the best I could
do.

The true story of a son who waited 70 years
in a church monastery in Southern Turkey for
his mother to come back.

Taken from Anatolian newspapers, a replicated
version to illustrate damages caused by war.

Educate, Some More?

Happily, I went to the market.
Sir may I say,
do you have some blueberries for
me in store today?

He came out and gave me
Raspberries, I said no.
Gooseberries, I said no.
Finally he said voila,
and showed up with the blackest
berries.

I said no.

He spent an half hour
or so,
he said madam a berry,
is a berry we got no more.
Why do you look so sore?

I said no.

Raspberries have brittle,
gooseberries have the bitterness of lead,
and black berries, as sweet as they may be,
will not go with my scone I just made.

Sadly I turn to the exit door,
before I leave,
may I educate you some more?
A berry is not a berry,
This is not what I was looking for.

The blues are not red, green or black.
Lastly all these flavours to me
are allergic, and wack.

Sir may I say, I am not sore,
The blues were the only ones
I was simply looking for.

Earthquake

The Gods are so mad
they cried.
Smoke is still spewing out
from its soil.
The earth has cracked
help us please.

We are transforming to human,
and just became humbled by the skies.
The grumbling of earth was so loud.
We are just starting to develop
consciousness.

The spirits did Jin, a form of
evil last night.
With us not knowing,
they were out in full disguise.

When we think about it.
Even beliefs were given
to us by the land and the seas.

We begged the different Gods to stop.
We have no clue,
why this has happened
to the innocence on earths as a being?

When the land moved,
there were so many gone.
We are still begging help
us please.

Split Soil Of An Earthquake

The Spanish Explorer

The Spanish explorer Alvaro de Mendana
de Neira in 1568 said:

*Smell the air by the sea
and feel this mist coming
down from the sky.*

*The Lord has delicately
blended in everything
so beautifully.*

*Tuvalu and Kiribati
should be known as
the land of
singing birds,
coconut milk and
beautiful half naked
Polynesian women.*

*We are hoping all
of them submit and comply.*

Kiribati Speaking Female

The Gods

I met all the Gods and they
had no color.
I met all the Gods and they
said we all have been moulded
from human designs.
I met all the Gods and they
whispered you are chosen.

I said to them but I am
a humble man from Bantu.
On this land I roam.
With waterbuck leather,
that is still stained with
dry blood on my back.

To others who asked
how I met all the Gods
I simply replied.

I merely looked at the moon
Over the, first Tombs of
Kings.
And simply saw them.

They even spoke to me.
I swore up and down,
I speak the truth.

Adamant I stand,
I met all the Gods.

I Meet All The Gods

Titanium

I am titanium made of an
unbroken will. But even
this strength sometimes fails to
go through the war.

On a cross that was meant
to lay.
The whips slash my body,
bloody becomes my soul.
My brain whispers through the torment.

Look at this ancient Forest,
and stay very still.
Hear their earliest noises.
Feel their spirits and don't fester.
You just got to ride the chi
of dark, a real life tester.

Let the eagle push
forth the power of wind.
Harness tightly its delicate
wings.

Start at zero,
wipe clean your gruesome past.
This pain beyond belief
that you thought permanent,
would surely not last.
This spell so obscure is really temporary.
Made from the dark clouds of
demonic evil exposed out from its sanctuary.

I now understand the concepts of life.
My existence has been made so great.
the titanium of my might.

Primeval Beech Forest

Evil Spirits

Evil has come to our region,
we had made into a home for centuries.
We carried an old aqueduct system at
close to 4500 years.
We had a well, pottery, tombs and a
Neolithic enclosure, called our earliest
settlements.

Our land and that of the neighbouring
regions became too violent. Food ran out.
We leave you behind Al Ain, an omen of
past
time.
We have opted to settle in Baluchistan
and will rebuild. We will now even do
the same type of pottery.

The evil spirits got the best of our region
and pray
these omen spirits to not follow us
through.

The Evil Spirits Of Al Ain

Evolutionary Difficulties

They were ok with Charles Darwin, but
they are not ok with me?

I stood in front of all the Royal Monarchs
And asked, "why can't you just let me be"?

I thought you favoured female leaders?
Don't you know shamans were once part
of thee?

The century is 21st and this is also your
lineage ancestry. Please try to see the
depth of our human evolutionary tree?

I am aware in modifying Darwin; the
world won't be same.
This was not guess work but rather the
study of social theories meant for humans
to gain.

I incorporated divine in all your pain.
It really isn't that hard if we simply
understand.

> "One by one Gods children came.
> All built by his loving hand.
> In the end the equation is simple.
> We were simply moulded to each section of
> earth as humans, let's try to be tame".

What makes you different from them,
is so easy to separate. Centuries later, you
had royals, they just had breaking of sticks
and
bare feet to navigate.

The Lady With The Lamp

Florence Nightingale we
call upon you,
we will send you over
with a team of 25.
Help our British soldiers in need.

In Istanbul you will be stationed
with them.
On the Asiatic side, where are men
will desperately need your hand.

The conditions are so unsanitary,
more assistance is needed,
a telegraph goes back.

I have decided to keep notes.
More have actually die from non-battle
related wounds than the ones who came
back from the Crimean war.

The regions are horribly suffering.
Overcrowding is severe,
we do have cholera outbreaks.
I am implementing organization
to the best of my ability.

We are trying to be human and
save all.

Nightingale In Istanbul, Turkey

The Light of Europe

Early in the 1800's,
at the height of its empire.
The British Dominion looked
beyond the seas.
They supported the base of Oxford
and knew to be progressive it had to be
strengthen.

Call it our interesting past.
The many Dukes and Duchess',
the irony of their vision of civility
that wanted to last.
Henry Morton Stanley, Henry Godwin,
and, Hugh Gough, to name just the few Sirs.

They said lets intricately study these
primitive foreign, make all their blood smear.
Merged secret alliances.
The treaties, of the many misunderstood
shamanic conceptions.
Bloodshed after bloodshed,
many enemies made them fear.

Out came enlightenment,
to the world they presented.
Little is advertise, how being better
at the time than the rest of the territories
that continuously attack.
Made them so Barbar resented.

Long hidden was their records of origin.
North Africa to Caucasus, we utter today.
Hey wait a minute Europe
that was your ancestral forefather's way.

*Humanity don't ever look cynical at our historical
past.*

When dark clouds of time comes, and
The Dominion enters hungry, the vast lands.
The question then posed was
"my clan or yours", only one can last.

The light of Europe shone.

The Light

Cock-Fighting

I am the Baron Rothschild Lionel of The East Indian Company, you need to entertain my team and I.

Alpha Quadrant

Once upon a time, when land was not owned. Caucasians lived in China and Asians in Europe.
Does this throw you off?

This is a true story in "defining human" of one researcher huff!
When the planet said that humans came from different sources. A correction was thought through.

These poems were written while under house arrest for telling academics understand clans for monkeys their dialogues is really something pertaining to all of you.

As numbers grew and darks clouds of time drew in. The land, became dominated.
Called a controlled territory this is how the story of unravelling all sorts of radicalization really begins.
§
Once upon a time, indigenous lived in Africa, but the same indigenous also lived in America.
Does this throw you off?

Columbus this time got confused and lumped all of them as shamanic Indian fools.
This is a true story regarding the difficulty one person had in explaining social variation through the simplest use, of the many fruits and berries. Oh the ridicule.
§
Once upon a time, more like a handful of years ago. North Africa to Anatolia was 600 years of one massive Ottoman linguistic pool.
Does this throw you off?
This is when no countries existed only a Sultan or two.

Do you know how all this research pass through?
I had to distribute my work for not being academic enough while I explained to them genetics, revolution of stars and how I could be the king's fool.

Star trek was visionary and futuristic you may or may not believe but in the end the world of technology, information and what is the Borg will be the very real analogy.

Kokopelli Tribe

To the sky's we blow a kiss.
Do you know us?
Root to skies we would say;

Kok or Gok
Gok or Kok

The dances of our forefathers,
feathers that are in disarray.
The symbol of fire.
Earthy spirits from terra,
lift us to the skies.

Kok or Gok
Gok or Kok

Blood we smear,
Nails we leave long.
Each scratch represents,
the number who have
died.

Kok or Gok
Gok or Kok

Skip around with might,
We do sounds for our dead.
Happy always is our tribe

*Kokopelli today translated from Anatolia to
across Central Turkic-Asian countries
means:*

"Kiss God's hand"

Native Kokopelli

The Other Side Of War

The struggle of human
is beyond belief.
The dry arid and painfully,
harsh deserts.

Our benefits at a
brutal cost.
The other side
that no one sees.

Giving benefits to those
on its own soil,
is as old as the first humans
that were born.

Give us moral and faith.
Stop fighting the same
team.
Everything you have is
because of a soldier's hope.

Behind the clouds,
a metal tag and a uniform outfit.
Given with such heartache.

A mother's wish and tears
for a better country.

Stuck At The Border

Mr. Officer I swear to you
I am innocent.
What's the big deal
They are only files
from a 100 years' old.

Linguistic anthropology
and technology.
What can I say?

They surrounded me with might.
I nibbled on my Smarties.
Want some? I teased?

Guess what Canada has
nothing that big,
I will fight for it back
vigilantly.
All these files belong to me.

I am better now.
Can you show some
neighbourly love?
 I know competition is your way
But this one is all of ours.
Please can there be no foul play.

Apache

Nomadic plains we travel.
Our language belongs to
the Athabaskan group.

We say one thing to the
white man only:

From man and women appeared both our
worlds.

Apache's Circle

Manhattan

Once upon a time
before the Empire State
building,
before the lights
and all the concrete.

There lived for centuries American
Natives on its soil.
They left many recipes, artefacts and
heritage things for settlers.
Most were claimed by others.

But their forefather's spirits in the skies kept
calling on earth,
the bones of our ancestral past.
Continuously praying for these
un-rested souls.

Just when humanity eradicated
everything due to our primitive past.
Scriptures were found so holy
even the biggest could not
cover the existence of the reminders
of their earliest cues.

They had no written but a
volcano of history may have
erupted with what was about to
be told.
The names,
of certain regions.
One that connects
the heart to the spirit
pounding in the skies.

We are here and still breathing,
but you can't see us.
The force of what is living is our
descriptive reminders,
of those that were unsaved.

How shall the unsaved ones escape back to
the heavens? The skies use to say.
If they are stuck between the earth and the
heavens.
Their neglected souls release should be
humanities "greatest of salvations".

Of that which was once done.
Our confusion regarding our hidden past.

Their protectorate of respect to the land and
no domination, an epoch of years of peaceful
existence.

An attempt by some to cover the sun
with clay for a temporary disguise.
So many generation of children.
The years that had all gone by.

These spirits continue their prayers.
Follow us we are here to guide you now, on
the eve of a warm summer celebration day
they sent wings from the skies.

"Learn from those who
have not rested.
Make amends with spirits
of what is living around you".
Let them break you free.

Unwell will become the people and the land,
our human connection to life, should be what
is in command.

Living is what we use to walked on.
This will start to transform its original
colors back to green from grey.

Learn the h-at-tan way. Another word for
beating life, of our Native spiritual ways.

I Am The Fallen Angel Lucifer

I want to be free,
free of any demise of even righteousness.
I want pleasure all the time.
I hate everything that is bound
by the laws of God.

I enjoy all the benefits that the darkness
designs.
Why do they try to box me or loathe me?
Not understanding the power of the
obscure
within me.
They have clipped my wings and I now
walk in human form.

I am the fallen angel Lucifer in disguise.

Lucifer With His Team

The Poisonous Shells

Oh spirits
The waters are so blue.
The land is so warm.
Yet we suffer so much.

Our ancestry use to say:

*"when sickness reaches and
destitute you have become"*

At low tide
go to the shores.

Find the poisonous shells.
The ones we dry out delicately,
with palm sticks and use for
décor.

And reincarnate without pain
back to earth for better more.

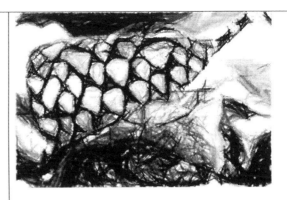

The Many Poisonous Shells

The Moon In The Day

I saw the white moon in the day
and asked, *"why did you shed your lunar color?"*

He responded, "it is to transcend further down towards the clouds and match their surroundings."

We came closer by climbing Nurata
and continued, *"why don't you join us here on*
earth, the leading light you are?"

The moon said "At 93 million miles, the distance to go back home would be far too great.
Its spirit must stay high, the light is the sensation we wish to give the eyes and most importantly
we are the ones that can emit colour?"

We will simply stay in our planetary system
and you can use us when darkness falls
and no other lights are there to help you.

The White Moon

V1- Vanuatu

Chief Roi Mata	
It does not matter how slowly I went, or the pain I felt upon departing. What matters is my eternal existence.	Roi

V2- Vatican City

Homage To The Sky	The hovering of air puff clouds, a peacock's tulle crown or a pink river dolphin. My soul pours out to you, how do you not even consider in thee?
Oh Atheist Oh Atheist How do you not believe in thee? See The glass butterfly, its protective wings made transparent. Delicately glass blown by the heavens above. Hear Oh Atheist Oh Atheist how do you not heart thee? The ocean waves lashing on the shores releasing sounds through vibrations of those living in it. Speak Oh Atheist Oh Atheist how do you not sense thee? The internal organs of man its life grown from specks of earth, in a shell of blood over thousands of years.	 Peacock's tulle crown

Caracas

The dark mountains we twirl around
the winding roads to the top.
The glassmaker sits patiently.
An indigenous trade-maker
heats the crystals carefully.
Out comes the blown glass.

He says "what would you like
me to make for you"?
Please sir pick anything.
Teach me everything
you know!

Well he blows gently and a spiral
of some sort of hot figurine
comes out.
Once upon a time
our elders also created art.

This form I built with my
hands may mean nothing
to you but it houses the spirits
of our first chiefs.

They once lived between tributaries
at the base of the mountains.
Their only fears were the visits
they would have to make.
Called the dark force of the mountain
tops.

Etched in design we kept their
different figurines made from
the land, close to us.

Take this back to Canada.
He lifts the figurine outside the
shed he works in,
and looks at the sky
of the mountain.

I just called for their spirits.
To be instilled in the glass.
It will protect you.
No money needed.
For remembering to preserve our history.
It is a gift from me to you.

Caracas Mountain Hilltop

Listen Only To Your Inner Soul

Vietnam also has an eye
in the sky, it watches them.
It says follow your conscious,
The delicate Feng shui principles,
your inner soul.

The voice of reason,
the thoughts of moral.
Nothing out beats
that of your divine purpose.

In the dark that voice
speaks to you.
God is you and your inner
soul.

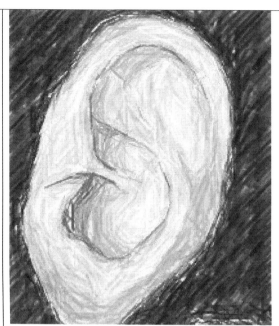

Listen To Your Inner Soul

Al- Yaman

An ancient culture, parked in the shores
by the Red sea.

They eventually made San'a their
fortified
place, a region at an altitude of 2,200m.
Situated in a mountain valley.

The few camel skin tent that were
covered
with greenery as camouflage for
those who may attack, was blended in.

At night there only entertainment
was sitting around a small fire
and recalling stories of old
proverbs, superstitions, mysticism
and poetry centuries old.

But even before trade took place
with the Babylonians and Egyptians.
Or the Islamic nomads of Arabia,
Jews or Shi'a from Persia
had move in.

They fed angrily the spirits of
those before them.
To the bastardized Gods they
would ululate and screech.

This one is for you.

Al- Yahman

-Z-

The Highest

The ancient doors.
The one whose light
shines glory.
We ask to be salvaged.

The womb in the sky responds,
Venus are the Gods,
A battle of lost, you seem to have endured
on earth the say.
What makes you wonder?

Twist of power has given way
based on the hardship of land,
the women say.

Horrid pain we feel.
We fight the realm
of struggle.
War leaves us destitute in appeal.
Deprivation, from the region of
Baal.

Ana, mother of all supreme.
Our confusion is unbearable.
We were the ones that created,
the lineage of concubines
of ancestry.
How we continued life, century after century,
why is this happening to thee?

Dark clouds continuously cover,
the seven mountainous tips.
The green gardens of the heaven
turned over all our keys.

Poverty has taken the better of us.
Covenant to God is no longer
part of us.
Send down a male, this time.
He will be God's child.

Power we will have to relent.
We will grab the children
and hope his wisdom can protect us.
A servitude of that to be reconciled.

Female Venus

Kariba

Our God is a black female
made from the region where women
go to consummate a marriage.

The blood that drips tells us,
their ancestry is now our ancestry.
The importance of the one that
gives life.

We make them compete so our
men become fierce.
We make them jealous so
our men get the best care.

And lastly we pray to them when
they died, our acknowledgement
that we are aware of their
spirits in the sky.

The Garden Region Of Consummation

Proof

51463997R00183